Bill Naismith is the series editor of the Fab̅␣␣␣l Guides. He was a Lecturer in Drama at the Un␣␣␣␣ f London, Goldsmiths' College, for twenty-five y␣␣␣ now lectures in Drama for the Central University ␣␣␣ in London. His other published work includes ␣␣␣ guides to *'Top Girls' by Caryl Churchill* (Methuen, *'The Rover' by Aphra Behn* (Methuen, 1993), *␣␣ Oka' by Robert Holman* (Methuen, 1994) and *␣␣ Country's Good' by Timberlake Wertenbaker* (Met␣ 1995).

FABER CRITICAL GUIDES
Series Editor: Bill Naismith

SAMUEL BECKETT
(*Waiting for Godot, Endgame, Krapp's Last Tape*)
by John Fletcher

BRIAN FRIEL
(*Philadelphia, Here I Come!, Translations, Making History,
Dancing at Lughnasa*)
by Nesta Jones

SEAN O'CASEY
(*The Shadow of a Gunman, The Plough and the Stars,
Juno and the Paycock*)
by Christopher Murray

TOM STOPPARD
(*Rosencrantz and Guildenstern Are Dead, Jumpers, Travesties,
Arcadia*)
by Jim Hunter

A FABER CRITICAL GUIDE
Harold Pinter

The Birthday Party
The Caretaker
The Homecoming

BILL NAISMITH

faber and faber

First published in 2000
by Faber and Faber Limited
3 Queen Square London WC1N 3AU

Photoset by Wilmaset Ltd, Birkenhead, Wirral
Printed in England by Mackays of Chatham plc, Chatham, Kent

A CIP record for this book
is available from the British Library
ISBN 0–571–19781–7

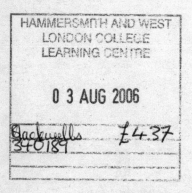
2 4 6 8 10 9 7 5 3

For Clare, Andrew, Rebecca and Ben

340189

Contents

Editor's Preface ix
Abbreviations x

Introduction
Pinter's Drama 1
Setting 3
Characterisation 6
Language 10
Early Life and Career 14

Context and Background 19
The New Companies 22
New Writing 25
Foreign Influences 29
Pinter and the New Writing 32

The Birthday Party
Synopsis 34
The Play 37
   The individual and society 37
   The play as metaphor 41
   Questions of identity 44
Characters 48
Dramatic Structure 56
Language 59
The Birthday Party: In Conclusion 72
Textual Notes 74

The Caretaker
Synopsis 87
The Play 90
   Realistic elements 91
   Comic elements 94
   Tragic elements 98
   Absurdist elements 101
Characters 104
Dramatic Structure 113
Language 116
The Caretaker: In Conclusion 124
Textual Notes 125

The Homecoming
Synopsis 132
The Play 136
   The family 138
   Ruth and the family 141
   The human jungle 149
   A comedy of bad manners? 152
   A sick enterprise? 156
Characters 158
Dramatic Structure 172
Language 177
   London speech 178
   The language of aggression 179
   The rhythm of Ruth 182
The Homecoming: In Conclusion 185
Textual Notes 186

Chronology of Plays 192
Select Bibliography 195

Editor's Preface

The *Faber Critical Guides* provide comprehensive introductions to major dramatists of the twentieth century.

The need to make an imaginative leap when reading
dramatic texts is well known. Plays are written with live
performance in mind. Often a theatre audience is confronted with a stage picture, a silent character or a vital
movement – any of which might be missed in a simple
'reading'. The *Guides* advise you what to look for.

All plays emerge from a context – a background – the
significance of which may vary but needs to be appreciated
if the original impact of the play is to be understood. A
writer may be challenging theatrical convention, reacting
to the social and political life of the time or engaging with
intellectual ideas. The *Guides* provide coverage of the
appropriate context in each case.

A number of key texts are examined in each *Guide* in
order to provide a sound introduction to the individual
dramatists. Studying only one work is rarely enough to
make informed judgements about the style and originality
of a writer's work. Considering several plays is also the
only way to follow a writer's development.

Finally, the *Guides* are meant to be read in conjunction
with the play texts. 'The play's the thing' and must always
be the primary concern. Not only are all playwrights
different but every play has its own distinctive features
which the *Guides* are concerned to highlight.

Abbreviations

Throughout this volume references are made to a number of other books on Pinter. Quotations are acknowledged in an abbreviated form in brackets, as follows:

Esslin, Martin, *Pinter the Playwright*, London: Methuen, 1992 (*Esslin*)

Gussow, M., *Conversations with Pinter*, London: Nick Hern Books, 1994 (*Gussow*)

Lahr, John, ed., *A Casebook on 'The Homecoming'*, New York: Grove Press, 1971 (*Lahr*)

Pinter, Harold, *Various Voices*, London: Faber and Faber, 1998 (*V.V.*)

Scott, Michael, ed., *Harold Pinter: 'The Birthday Party', 'The Caretaker' and 'The Homecoming': A Casebook*, London: Macmillan, 1986 (*Casebook*)

All quotations and page references from the three plays that are the subject of this book are taken from the new single editions of the plays published by Faber and Faber in 2000.

I am grateful to Anthony Cunningham, Steven Dykes and Geoffrey James for their help and advice during the preparation of this book. – B.N.

Introduction

Pinter's Drama

The Birthday Party flopped when first performed in London in 1958, taken off by the producers after only one week in response to a generally unfavourable press. However, the highly respected critic Harold Hobson recognised a significant voice and claimed that the play's author 'possesses the most original, disturbing and arresting talent in theatrical London'. *The Caretaker* was a great success in 1960 and established Harold Pinter as a major dramatist of the newly burgeoning English theatre. When *The Homecoming* opened in London in 1965 the critic Penelope Gilliatt was entirely convinced, recognising 'a man in total command of his talent'.

Pinter has continued to work in all aspects of theatre, as dramatist, actor and director; and he has written for radio and most impressively for film, where he has become recognised as a master of adaptation for films which include *The Servant*, *Accident*, *The Go-Between* and *The French Lieutenant's Woman*. As a dramatist he has gained national and international recognition unequalled among his contemporaries. His plays are performed world-wide and are regularly revived, each new work being eagerly anticipated. The three full-length plays which are the subject of this volume are now firmly established as classics of twentieth-century English theatre; they made

Pinter's reputation and in them can be found the essential features of his style and dramaturgy.

The plays have inspired a vast amount of scholarly criticism and analysis which immediately suggests that there is a lot to be said about them, that they are some-how significantly different from other people's work, and that they are open to a variety of interpretations. As a starting point it might be asked: why should plays that initially seem very conventional, almost old-fashioned in their appearance, be regarded as original, fresh and dis-turbing? How is it that they retain the interest of both audiences and theatre practitioners, especially actors? What is new?

Pinter spent a number of years as an actor before he began writing plays, mostly touring and working in repertory during the 1950s, and so became closely acquainted with the conventions of the 'well made' rep. play, the staple diet of small-town provincial England. Whether it were a country-house thriller or a more sophisticated Terence Rattigan work, certain essentials were taken for granted in these plays: characters in modern dress, in recognisable relationships, speaking a language that everybody could understand, all set in a domestic interior. These conventions of simple natural-ism, where everything appears to reflect normal life, extend back to the nineteenth century and were adopted by most European and American playwrights as well as English. Plays as different as Henrik Ibsen's *A Doll's House*, Arthur Miller's *All My Sons* and Arnold Wesker's *Roots* all present a visual stage picture reflecting the life of their time. Pinter adopted his own experience without much question: 'Whenever I write for the stage I merely see the stage I've been used to . . . I always think of the

normal picture-frame stage which I used as an actor.'
Early in his career he even claimed that 'I regard myself as
an old-fashioned writer' (*Casebook*, p. 31). However,
what distinguishes Pinter is the extent to which he *stylises*
all the most familiar conventions of this stage – the
treatment of stage setting, personal relationships (which
involve 'character') and language. In his plays these
conventions are heightened, intensified and taken beyond
what is normally expected of everyday events.

Pinter has commented on all these aspects of his work,
and while it is wise to heed D. H. Lawrence's warning
'trust the tale, not the teller', Pinter has made fascinating
observations about his approach to character and
language on stage which are indeed useful. On the one
hand Pinter became almost notorious for refusing to
elucidate his work in public or to reveal answers to the
mysteries which are contained within it: 'I can sum up
none of my plays. I can describe none of them, except to
say: That is what happened. That is what they said. That is
what they did' (*V.V.*, p. 34). On the other hand Pinter's
career has extended over a very long time during which he
has given the occasional speech or interview which *is*
revealing and all the more intriguing because of the
relative rarity of such statements. Pinter has advanced and
developed long-established theatrical conventions and
how he has done so might be examined in the light of
his own opinions, under the separate headings of *setting*,
characterisation and *language*.

Setting

The curtains of the proscenium arch stage have invariably
opened on a scene of domesticity. The setting within a

house provides a serviceable environment for the action but also, crucially, helps to define the social standing of those who live in it. Sometimes these rooms may contain highly significant or even symbolic features (such as the portrait of General Gabler in Ibsen's *Hedda Gabler*, the votive light in Sean O'Casey's *Juno and the Paycock*, or the bookcases in Eugene O'Neill's *Long Day's Journey Into Night*), but for the most part this stage setting is a 'given' – something we take for granted – and our attention is directed entirely towards the relationships between the characters on stage. How much the conventional naturalistic set is a 'given' is shown in a brief extract of the stage description for Granville-Barker's *The Voysey Inheritance*:

> The Voysey dining-room at Chislehurst, when children and grandchildren are visiting, is dining-table and very little else. And at the moment in the evening when five or six men are sprawling back in their chairs, and the air is clouded with smoke, it is a *very typical* specimen of the English middle-class domestic temple. It has *the usual* red-papered walls, *the usual* varnished woodwork which is known as grained oak; there is *the usual* hot, mahogany furniture; and, commanding point of the whole room, there is *the usual* black-marble sarcophagus of a fireplace . . .

In Pinter's early plays the stage setting, 'the room', approximates to photographic realism, but it takes on a heightened significance. The stage space literally defines the living perimeters of the inhabitants, and the action of the play, in part, focuses on who is in control of the room. The stage becomes the territorial space in which characters try to dominate and take, or keep, possession.

Pinter has often explained that his plays begin with an image he has experienced, something that he has seen which plants a seed:

I have usually begun a play in quite a simple manner; found a couple of characters in a particular context, thrown them together and listened to what they said, keeping my nose to the ground . . . I've never started a play from any kind of abstract idea or theory. (*V.V.*, p. 17)

The 'particular context' has always been a room, and the room has a door. 'Two people in a room – I am dealing a great deal of the time with this image of two people in a room. The curtain goes up on the stage, and I see it as a very potent question: What is going to happen to those two people in the room? Is someone going to open the door and come in?' We all live in rooms which contain our possessions and reflect our personal interests. If we invite people into our house/flat/room it is usually with a tacit understanding that the guest will leave at a suitable moment. If they don't or won't we are likely to be in trouble. Edward Albee's play *A Delicate Balance* explores this dilemma, when visitors refuse to leave, and other plays make the intrusion of a stranger the subject of the drama – J. B. Priestley's *An Inspector Calls*, for example.

Many of Pinter's plays develop from the moment of intrusion, when privacy has been invaded and a threatening situation ensues. This is the subject of his first play, significantly titled *The Room* (directed by Henry Woolf in 1957), which is set in a room of a large house. Rose is excessively conscious of the importance to her of the room: 'No, this room's all right for me. I mean, you know where you are' . . . 'If they ever ask you, Bert, I'm quite happy where I am' . . . 'This is a good room. You've got a chance in a place like this.' Eventually a stranger enters, with violent consequences. The action in *The Birthday Party*, *The Caretaker* and *The Homecoming* is provoked, in each case, by strangers intruding into a private space. In these plays it is the sheer ordinariness of the setting which makes the action the more fearful when the intrusion occurs. In later plays such as *Old Times* and *No Man's Land*, where the domestic setting is much more up-market and middle-class, the formula of intrusion into a space and a relationship is the same.

Critics often remark on the fight for territory, for possession of the space, which provides much of the subtext in Pinter, but clearly there is more at stake than simple territory, however much it is coveted. The behaviour of the characters, their defensive tactics and how they react physically and verbally when confronted with a vital challenge holds our theatrical attention. The repetition of this scenario: a character – or two characters (as in *The Birthday Party*) – intruding as some kind of threat into a very private, personal situation might even be regarded as a metaphor. It is evidence for what Pinter perceives as a general state: that is, the essential isolation of the individual and his wish to avoid communication with the outside world.

Characterisation

Pinter's approach to characterisation is well documented and needs to be considered. For some time he was criticised for deliberate obscurity, in offering contradictory information about characters or no information at all: as if he were not playing fair with the audience. Why, for example, has Goldberg got three names in *The Birthday Party*? And what kind of wife and mother was Jessie in *The Homecoming*? Many familiar plays and playwrights provide an exposition early on which informs audiences of how characters are related and convention dictates what their dramatic function will be. In some cases a character is fulfilling a 'thematic' function, which is their main purpose. This can be found in the work of Bernard Shaw, in *Major Barbara* for example, where characters often speak for one side of an argument or another. Or in David Hare's trilogy on Thatcher's England – *Racing Demon*, *Aspects of War* and *Murmuring Judges* – where most of the characters are 'representative'. The function of characters in *Murmuring Judges*, is, basically, to represent the constabulary, members of the Bench and Bar, the prison service, the Government and clients of the legal profession, in order to present an overview of the state of the legal profession in contemporary Britain. Pinter doesn't do this. His approach to 'character' has a different starting point.

Pinter has explained that his writing process is one of 'finding out' about his characters by following how they proceed from his initial image of them. But this is not an arbitrary process or one that leads to 'Absurd' theatre, where characters do not conform to recognisable psychological behaviour. Crucially, Pinter believes 'It's a good part for an actor if the character possesses a proper and full life', and all actors, some of whom may have had initial difficulties understanding where their character has come from, attest to how marvellous they are to play. Paul Rogers, who first played Max in *The Homecoming*, recognised the actor's instinct and experience behind the writing – 'A nonacting playwright can be a very responsible writer, but he doesn't have the feeling for the ultimate enjoyment of the performer. One is absolutely sure Pinter would be delighted to play any single character in his plays.' This is an important clue to the effectivness in the theatre of the long set speeches – or monologues – in the plays, which allow, in part, for virtuoso performances. There is a psychologic to how characters speak and behave in Pinter, but not everything is explained in an obvious way. As Paul Rogers says, 'The wonderful thing about Pinter is that he really writes about people. And the extraordinary way in which ordinary people's minds work. Ordinary people don't behave like people in a well-made play, where you follow one line of direction.'

From a psychoanalytical point of view, Pinter is an acute observer of human behaviour and is well aware that the individual psyche is very complex and does not always operate according to reason. In particular, the individual in the present is affected by his experiences in the past, which cannot easily be defined with certainty. From Pinter's point of view the past is a continuous mystery, a place where both good and bad experiences can be remembered, more or less vaguely, and which leaves us in the present in a state of insecurity. Personal insecurity leads many of Pinter's characters to devious evasions, linguistic strategies to protect themselves, or language games. This makes the conventional 'character study' much more difficult in the plays of Pinter – because characters don't wish to be 'known', and rarely offer a convincing explanation of themselves. The question of individual 'identity' becomes a central issue in the plays.

A clue to Pinter's approach to characterisation may be found in the list of characters, the *dramatis personae*, which precedes each printed text or is given in theatre programmes. What is consistently given is the age and sex of the character, nothing more. In *The Homecoming* we see that Teddy is 'a man in his middle thirties', Ruth is 'a woman in her early thirties'. We are not told that they are married. We are not told that Mick and Aston are brothers in *The Caretaker*. It is usual for such a list to identify connections, especially family relationships. What can be deduced from Pinter's lack of information? Given that the relationships are absolutely vital to an understanding of behaviour, and that Pinter knows full well what the relationships are – why not tell us? Perhaps the information lies indeed at the heart of the plays. The unfolding drama of each play is an ongoing process of exploring *how* we relate to other people, and what the true extent of an actual relationship is. Pinter's method of instinctively responding to his characters as he writes allows for this revelation of truths about human relationships.

In this enquiry, consistently in Pinter's plays, the family and family relationships emerge as a fundamental social unit. Outside the family nobody relates intimately, and within the family relationships are unavoidable but, as often as not, fraught. The ambivalence of family relationships is a central theme in many of the plays. *The Caretaker* depends for its logical action on the fact that Aston and Mick are brothers. In *The Homecoming* the action calls into question whether the 'marriage' of Teddy and Ruth means anything at all. In *Landscape* a husband and wife inhabit quite different imaginative worlds. In *The Birthday Party*, through the character of Goldberg, the family is seen as part of an oppressive and demanding system. In *Family Voices* a mother and son talk to each other but are widely separated and have been for ages.

Language

The language of Pinter's plays is their most distinctive feature and here, by general consent, is to be found their most profound originality. Pinter's concern for language is paramount. His style has become instantly recognisable and, perhaps uniquely, a page of a Pinter text even looks like nobody else's. Dialogue is invariably sparse, interspersed with pauses and silences, and broken up with a lengthy set speech. Mr Kidd in *The Room* says of the mysterious Riley: 'he won't indulge in any conversation'. But in Pinter hardly anybody ever does. Characters engage in dialogue, and the dialogue and speeches in Pinter have sharpened and even revised our awareness of how people engage in speech both on and off the stage.

Pinter's early plays were accompanied by a number of theatre review sketches which were very popular in the 1960s. In sketches such as 'The Black and White', 'Request Stop' and 'Last to Go', the idiosyncrasies of English discourse were exposed, mainly for comic effect. Pinter was acknowledged to have a remarkable 'ear' for the rhythm and quirkiness of English speech, notably as employed by lower-class, less-educated people in London. The odd cadences, pregnant pauses, repetition and non-sequiturs contributed to the claim that Pinter's language has a tape-recorder accuracy, but in fact there was always a degree of stylisation involved – as here, when two old women are sitting at a milk bar table:

SECOND: . . . I see you talking to two strangers as I come in. You want to stop talking to strangers, old piece of boot like you, you mind who you talk to.
FIRST: I wasn't talking to any strangers.

Pause. The FIRST OLD WOMAN *follows the progress of a bus through the window.*
That's another all-night bus gone down. (*Pause*)
Going up the other way. Fulham way. (*Pause*) That was a two-nine-seven. (*Pause*) I've never been up that way. (*Pause*) I've been down to Liverpool Street.
SECOND: That's up the other way.
FIRST: I don't fancy going down there, down Fulham way, and all up there.
SECOND: Uh-uh.
FIRST: I've never fancied that direction much.
Pause.
SECOND: How's your bread?
Pause.
FIRST: Eh?
SECOND: Your bread.
FIRST: All right. How's yours?
Pause.
SECOND: They don't charge for the bread if you have soup.

('The Black and White')

In the full-length plays there is much comedy to be derived from our recognition of these speech patterns but this generally gives way to a more serious consideration of language strategies when characters become competitive or threatened, as Pinter is well aware – 'on the whole, the laughter goes out of any play I've written before it's finished. I can't think of any play of mine in which there are really any laughs at all in the last ten minutes.'

Where Pinter has created an original style of dramatic dialogue is in his departure from the conventional notion that characters on stage must be articulate and able to converse in perfectly formed sentences. Underlying this idea is the reasonable assumption that characters on stage are content to be talking to each other – they are not self-conscious about it. Pinter has always argued from a different perspective. In a famous remark he claims, 'One way of looking at speech is to say that it is a constant stratagem to cover nakedness' and, he goes on 'I think that we communicate only too well, in our silence, in what is unsaid, and that what takes place is a continual evasion, desperate rearguard attempts to keep ourselves to ourselves. Communication is too alarming. To enter into someone else's life is too frightening. To disclose to others the poverty within us is too fearsome a possibility' (*V.V.*, p. 20). Consequently much of the dialogue in a Pinter play is strategic, a means of self-protection. Characters are frequently acting in self-defence or are seeking to domin-ate (which is another form of self-defence). Stanley, in *The Birthday Party*, is always speaking from a position of defensive panic; Davies, in *The Caretaker*, after years of evasion, is incapable of giving a straight reply to a straight question and often he cannot finish a sentence; Lenny, in *The Homecoming*, is constantly speaking in a devious manner in order to impose himself.

The difficulties that characters experience with lan-guage are underlined by the pauses and silences for which Pinter's dialogue has become renowned. These breaks in fluent speech are marked on the printed page in three ways. A speech can be broken by three dots, or by the stage directions *Pause* or *Silence*. These pauses always contribute to the rhythm of the dialogue, but equally naturally they also indicate something of what is going on. As Pinter describes the function of these linguistic devices, 'The pause is a pause because of what has just happened in the minds and guts of the characters. They spring out of the text. They're not formal conveniences or stresses but part of the body of the action. And a silence equally means that something has happened to create the impossibility of anyone speaking for a certain amount of time – until they can recover from whatever happened before the silence' (*Gussow*, p. 36).

Many characters in the naturalist tradition, when confined for three or four acts in one small space for a limited time, resort to reminiscence. This is invariably their method of self-justification, of explaining themselves as they are in the present. Locked in the confined stage space, they often resort to stories. In Strindberg's *Miss Julie*, for example, the manservant Jean is asked to tell of his first love and he replies, 'That was the story I wouldn't tell you a few minutes ago, but now I'm going to', and he does. Later, after Jean has made love to Miss Julie, she says, 'We'll run away; but we must talk it over first. At least I must – so far you've done all the talking. You've told me all about your life – now I'm going to tell you mine', and she does. Miller's Willy Loman, in *Death of a Salesman*, pleads to his employer, 'Just let me tell you a story, Howard', in order to justify himself. In Osborne's *Look Back in Anger* the characters do a lot of 'looking back' and much of the play is in the past tense. Storytelling and characters reminiscing is an accepted convention in drama. But part of the convention is that we in the audience are expected to believe what we are told, and usually we are right to do so. In Pinter the situation is different.

It is a marked convention in Pinter's plays that characters reminisce or tell stories, but the truthful re-counting of past events cannot be relied on. Always these stories are strategic, part of the ongoing process of establishing domination in a relationship or of surviving in a competition of egos. Goldberg, Mick and Lenny all have set-piece speeches which 'use' the past for present purposes, and these will be considered in due course. It is very important, however, when reading Pinter and when confronted with one of these set speeches, which often include bizarre and brilliantly inventive flights of imagination, to ask the question – why is the character saying this? What is the immediate purpose? There is always a reason for the speeches, which might be regarded as 'fictional reminiscence'. In Pinter's later plays his characters tend to be more educated and more articulate, but they engage in linguistic strategies just the same, and stories are a part of an ongoing confrontation. This deliberate use of a stylised language is explained by Anna in *Old Times*, who competes with Deeley throughout the play with stories intended to better their standing with Kate: '. . . I do know what you mean. There are some things one remembers even though they may never have happened. There are things I remember which may never have happened but as I recall them so they take place.'

Early Life and Career

In the case of Harold Pinter it is possible to see connections between his early life, his formative career in the theatre, and his work as a dramatist.

To begin with the facts, Pinter was born in Hackney, East London, in 1930, the only child of a Jewish tailor. At the beginning of World War II (1939) he experienced, at an early age, two periods of evacuation, firstly to Cornwall and then nearer to London. Between 1942 and

1948 he attended Hackney Downs Grammar School (for boys) where he excelled in English and drama (playing the lead parts of Macbeth and Romeo in school plays), and sport. After school he attended the Royal Academy of Dramatic Art for a brief time (dropping out after two terms). He registered as a conscientious objector when called up for military service and had two tribunals/trials which might easily have put him in prison. In both cases he was fined. After another brief period of actor-training he joined Anew McMaster's Theatre Company and toured Ireland for a year, acting in eleven plays – seven of which were by Shakespeare. In 1953 he played in eight productions in Donald Wolfit's company. His life as an actor, under the stage-name David Baron, continued between 1954 and 1959 in repertory theatres throughout Britain. In 1956 he married the actress Vivien Merchant, and they had a son in 1958. Pinter's first play, *The Room*, was written for a friend, Henry Woolf, who directed and acted in it at Bristol University. Thereafter plays for theatre, radio and television followed at regular intervals. Pinter acted in some and directed others, and he began his career as a writer of film scripts in 1963, when he adapted both *The Caretaker* and *The Servant* (directed by Joseph Losey). In 1966, the year after *The Homecoming* was first performed, he was awarded the CBE in recognition of his playwriting.

This bald summary, up to 1966, carries with it significant details that have shaped Pinter's life and work. To begin with, being born Jewish in East London and to experience World War II at close hand, was to have life-long consequences. Not only was London in the front line of attack and regular bombing an event that was either experienced directly or heard about while evacuated, but Fascist anti-Semitism was a reality in East London even after the war. Pinter experienced violence from this source on the streets of Hackney. The threat and actuality of violence, symbolised by the German Gestapo and carried on after the war, became a part of a general consciousness – a permanent scar on the mind. The threat of violence, from unspecified 'authorities', is reflected in some of Pinter's early plays, which have been called 'Comedies of Menace'. *The Dumb Waiter*, *The Hothouse* and *The Birthday Party* can readily be seen as metaphors for political aggression against the individual. Furthermore, Pinter's refusal to join the army, so soon after the war, is indicative of his independent spirit and moral awareness. He simply found the idea of another war 'immoral', and his radical rejection of official brutality and oppression has been carried through to his later plays and his activities in support of persecuted writers worldwide.

From a different perspective, Pinter's writing has inevitably been influenced by his education and experience of living in East-End Hackney. Pinter acknowledges the inspirational influence of his English teacher Joseph Brearley, who remained a friend after Pinter left school. Pinter began writing poetry at an early age but Brearley broadened his experience of English literature, which has remained an abiding passion. And this interest in the written word was augmented by the everyday experience of the language of the street which, in post-war East London, was rich and energetic and used with relish: it is clearly reflected in the expression of a line of Pinter characters, including Goldberg, Davies and Max.

Pinter's experience as an actor was the best possible apprenticeship for a dramatist, in so far as he absorbed naturally all that holds an audience in the theatre in terms of structure, performance, speech and movement. It is, perhaps, not a freakish coincidence that so many of our greatest modern playwrights did not receive a university education. John Osborne, Tom Stoppard, Edward Bond and Harold Pinter (all extremely well-read) derived their creative Muse not from theory but from practice. Some commentators have seen an inspirational influence in the talent of Pinter's first wife, Vivien Merchant, who acted in many of his plays and who was an outstanding Ruth in *The Homecoming*. Not only was she technically brilliant but she possessed, as an actress, an aura of enigmatic and stylish sexuality and a stillness which perfectly suited many of his female roles.

Pinter has continued to work in all areas of theatre, as writer, actor and director. His full list of plays is included in Chapter Six. His career has been recognised and honoured in quite unprecedented terms at home and abroad: as well as the CBE awarded in 1966, he has been awarded the Shakespeare Prize (Hamburg); the European Prize for Literature (Vienna); the Pirandello Prize (Palermo); and the David Cohen British Literature Prize. He has been awarded honorary doctorates from a range of universities at home and abroad and he is an honorary fellow of Queen Mary College, London. He has also been awarded the Laurence Olivier Special Award and the Molière d'Honneur in Paris in recognition of his life's work. The BBC celebrated Pinter's sixtieth birthday with a whole evening on Radio 3 dedicated to his work, and the University of Ohio held an international conference in his honour. Festivals in his name were held in Barcelona in 1996 and in Dublin in 1994 and 1997. An annual *Pinter Review*, published by the University of Tampa Press, is dedicated to his work. Pinter still lives in London and is now married to Lady Antonia Fraser.

Note

There is a vast amount of scholarly criticism on Pinter's work and some of the most interesting books are detailed at the end of this volume. However, there are two books, readily available in paperback, that make very useful introductions and commentaries on the writer and his work, covering his entire career. These are Martin Esslin's *Pinter the Playwright* (Methuen, 1973, revised 1992) and Michael Billington's *The Life and Work of Harold Pinter* (Faber, 1996).

Context and Background

The impact of Pinter's early plays and the critical reaction to them – which varied from welcoming excitement to resentment and confusion – was determined by the theatrical context in which they were written. That is, the late 1950s and early 1960s, which were, in theatrical terms, very different from now. It is perhaps confusing to regard Pinter as a significant contemporary writer of that time when he is unquestionably still a major contemporary writer today, because the context has changed so much and his impact then was of a different kind to his impact now. His early work presented an original style and an approach to plays which was challenging, and to an extent controversial; forty years later, his achievements and reputation always command serious attention. One reason for Pinter's continued appeal has been his steady development over the years in both style and subject matter. However, it is important to recognise that *The Birthday Party*, *The Caretaker* and *The Homecoming* were remarkable plays partly because they were each so different from the typical theatre of their time.

When Pinter entered the profession as an actor in the early 1950s the theatrical 'map' in Britain was very restricted. Theatre was a commerical business, run for profit, providing entertainment and dependent on star performers. There was no English Stage Company at the Royal Court Theatre, no Royal Shakespeare Company, no National Theatre, no subsidy as we know it today (the budget of the Arts Council rarely supported new work), and no 'fringe' theatre in London. Furthermore, there was no formal theatre in education, no public examinations at GCSE or 'A' Level in Theatre Studies, no drama departments in any of our universities. Live performance was of no academic interest.

Certainly the classics were performed in London and by touring companies (Pinter toured in Shakespeare and Sophocles), but the quality of 'new' playwriting was lamented by serious observers. Kenneth Tynan, who was to gain a reputation as the most gifted post-war theatre critic and who became the first Literary Manager of the National Theatre, was wholly embarrassed by the state of British playwriting in 1955:

> The bare fact is that, apart from revivals and imports, there is nothing in the London theatre that one dares discuss with an intelligent man for more than five minutes. Since the great Ibsen challenge of the nineties, the English intellectuals have been drifting away from drama. Synge, Pirandello and O'Casey briefly recaptured them, and they will still perk up at the mention of Giraudoux. But – cowards – they know Eliot and Fry only in the study; and of a native prose playwright who might set the boards smouldering they see no sign at all. (*Tynan on Theatre*, Penguin, 1961, p. 31)

Tynan was crusading for a new and vital theatre which might be seriously involved with social and political matters of the day – and he championed it when it arrived – so the absence of new writing led him perhaps to underestimate the 'style' which could be found in revivals of Shaw or in the work of Coward, Rattigan and Anouilh in the 1950s. The period was not entirely a wasteland.

London had seen the best plays of Tennessee Williams and Arthur Miller; poetic drama was, perhaps, esoteric and not popular, but musicals were stylish and a real delight. Also Joan Littlewood was working, maverick-like, in the East End of London with her Theatre Workshop.

Kenneth Tynan was, in the main, regretting the absence of serious 'content' in plays that were little more than a fashionable diversion. Plays did not reflect the contemporary life of Britain. He was also speaking, most significantly as it turned out, on behalf of the younger generation who were deeply disenchanted with post-war Britain and whose voice was absent from the theatre. The theatrical scene was to change radically in the next few years, to the extent that vivid terms such as 'renaissance', even 'revolution', have been applied to the events that occurred between 1955 and the mid-1960s, coinciding exactly with the arrival of Pinter as a dramatist. As a measure of the change that was to occur in the British theatre in the later part of the century, we can compare Tynan's lament that in 1955 there was not *one* new writer worth mentioning, or even in sight, with the catalogue of a British Council exhibition entitled *Contemporary British Dramatists* in 1992, which features no less than sixty-six writers seriously worthy of attention (none of whom were known in 1955). Something must have happened.

The change that has come about in the latter half of the century was begun in the late 1950s and early 1960s. Most importantly an opportunity was provided for new writing by the establishment of new theatre companies in search of plays.

The New Companies

1956 is commonly regarded as a milestone in the history of modern drama because in that year John Osborne's *Look Back in Anger* was first performed, and drew attention to the English Stage Company which had taken up residence at the Royal Court Theatre in Sloane Square, London. From that date until now the Royal Court has maintained a reputation for championing new writers and, whatever the quality of acting and design, it has always been 'the writer' who has had priority when artistic decisions have been made. Following the success of Osborne's early plays, a succession of new names were introduced to the English theatre. Pinter's *The Room* and *The Dumb Waiter* were performed there in 1960.

Most of the writers whose contemporary plays fill the theatre shelves of major bookshops at the end of the century have been performed at the Royal Court. In the early days – as well as Osborne – John Arden, Arnold Wesker, Joe Orton and Edward Bond were all closely linked with this theatre. There was never any sense of their being a 'group', but they each fulfilled the criteria of the Artistic Director, George Devine, that theatre should be 'part of the intellectual life of the community', and that plays should be immediately relevant. Devine wanted a theatre which was not dedicated only to the West End idea of success – which was star names and long runs. He was prepared to grant his writers 'the right to fail'; by which was meant that success was not to be measured solely by the box office. None of John Arden's plays made any money at the Royal Court.

It was soon apparent that here was a stage where new voices were able to comment on the state of Britain. These were generally young voices, largely anti-establishment and prepared to shock. They were frequently in conflict with the official censor, the office of the Lord Chamberlain, and by 1968 such was the support gained by the quality of new dramatic writing that the Government succumbed and censorship was removed from the English theatre. Osborne and Bond in particular were regularly in trouble with the Lord Chamberlain, and the Royal Court occasionally turned itself into a private club in order to show their work. In his role as the official 'censor', the Lord Chamberlain was effectively keeping a grip on what the establishment held most dear. The Church and the Royal Family were sacrosanct and virtually unmentionable, Government ministers hardly less so; displays of violence and, especially, sexual behaviour, were unacceptable. Most disturbing to the new playwrights, obviously, was the puritanical curb on language, notably sexual language. Pinter had to wait a long time to have *The Homecoming* accepted, and he had to accept some cuts (now happily restored).

Perhaps a signal of the rapid change in what was being staged at this period becomes evident in the year 1958. During this year some of the new plays – each very different – included Samuel Beckett's *Krapp's Last Tape*, Shelagh Delaney's *A Taste of Honey*, Ann Jellicoe's *The Sport of My Mad Mother*, Pinter's *The Birthday Party*, Arnold Wesker's *Chicken Soup With Barley* and Peter Shaffer's *Five Finger Exercise*. This same year saw the production of Terence Rattigan's *Variation on a Theme*, which failed, and terminated this dramatist's long run of success with the middle-class audiences he was so adept at pleasing. The dominant post-war theatre of character and narrative, set in an unchallenging middle-class environment, was under serious threat.

Soon after the Royal Court Theatre became the unofficial centre of new writing, the two major British theatre companies were established, both of which provided a stage for new plays. In 1960, Peter Hall transformed the Stratford Memorial Theatre (hitherto used for a summer festival of Shakespeare productions, led by starry actors) into the Royal Shakespeare Company, with profound implications for the British theatre in general. This is not the appropriate place to describe in detail all the innovations of the new regime, which included the recruitment of academically trained directors who elevated the status of 'the text' over the attraction of star actors; the virtual creation of 'directors' theatre, which has dominated our bigger companies ever since; the notion of a permanent 'ensemble', who could develop a 'style' of performance under the security of long-term contracts; and the imposition of a production 'aesthetic', whereby all aspects of production – acting, costume, sound and set design – could be unified in relation to an understanding of the play text. All this quickly raised the profile of classic theatre in Britain, and changed the overall map, but it had no direct influence on the work of Harold Pinter. What pertains to the plays of Pinter is that Peter Hall quickly decided to broaden the activities of the company, and he took over the Aldwych Theatre in London as a base for the production of plays, old and new, which were not by Shakespeare, in order to enlarge the acting experience of his company. Once established in London, the Royal Shakespeare Company soon gained a reputation for radical new work, much of it quite shocking – and far removed from Shakespeare. Peter

Brook's version of the *Marat/Sade*, John Whiting's *The Devils* and David Rudkin's *Afore Night Come* were all radical and disturbing in their subject matter. Pinter's *The Homecoming*, directed very successfully by Peter Hall in 1965, established Pinter as one of the company's major playwrights.

In 1962, Laurence Olivier, the country's most illustrious actor, opened the National Theatre as its Artistic Director at the Old Vic Theatre in London. This company was also created on the principle of an ensemble and, without the imposition of Shakespeare as house dramatist, it very sensibly settled for no more specific an artistic policy than to produce the best plays of all time in the best possible way. The company also provided the opportunity for contemporary writers to be given excellent productions. Peter Shaffer, Tom Stoppard and John Arden were all performed by the National Theatre early on. Later, when Peter Hall replaced Olivier, Pinter's new work was performed by the National (eventually to become the Royal National Theatre) on the South Bank in London. In 1973, Pinter was to become an associate director.

New Writing

A catalogue of the plays produced between 1956 and 1965 shows a very impressive variety of written style in the work of Arden, Osborne, Beckett, Pinter, Wesker, Shaffer and Orton; and from 1962 Edward Bond became an increasingly important figure, making politics a serious theme in contemporary drama. What emerged as the essential and radical contribution of many of these playwrights was the uncompromising expression of discontent with contemporary Britain. The new theatrical voices were predominantly young, and they captured the imagination of the younger generation who became interested in the theatre as never before. The sound of youthful characters giving ardent expression to their anger and frustration at the failure of Britain to revive and transform after the Second World War was somewhat patronisingly greeted by the older generation of theatre critics. Jimmy Porter – the original angry young man – was found to be 'numbing' by the *Manchester Guardian*'s reviewer when he saw *Look Back in Anger* in 1956:

> Mr Osborne's hero, a boor, a self-pitying, self-dramatising intellectual rebel who drives his wife away, takes a mistress and then drops her when, to his surprise, his wife comes crawling back, will not be thought an edifying example of chivalry.

Kenneth Tynan, a critic of the younger generation, was more concerned with the fact that Jimmy Porter was 'simply and abundantly alive; that rarest of dramatic phenomena, the act of original creation, has taken place; and those who carp were better silent'. Jimmy represented 'post-war youth as it really is' – and Tynan estimated the number in Britain, aged between twenty and thirty, at nearly seven million. He welcomed this dramatic expression of genuine feeling:

> All the qualities are there, qualities one had despaired of ever seeing on the stage – the drift towards anarchy, the instinctive leftishness, the automatic rejection of 'official' attitudes, the surrealist sense of humour (Jimmy describes a pansy friend as 'a female Emily Brontë'), the casual promiscuity, the sense of lacking a

crusade worth fighting for and, underlying all these, the determination that no one who dies shall go unmourned.

Osborne's next play, *The Entertainer* (1957), was equally damning of contemporary Britain, which was depicted as tatty and in decline through the experience of the failing music-hall comedian Archie Rice. Osborne was to open a floodgate of impassioned denunciation of official and establishment attitudes. In particular, the cause of the working class was given articulate and unsentimental expression, virtually for the first time on the modern English stage, by writers such as Arden, Orton and Wesker. Wesker's 'Trilogy' of plays set in London's East End is a personal indictment of how the working class have allowed themselves to be duped. His heroine in *Roots*, Beatie Bryant, finally speaks out to her working-class family against the cheap commercialism that keeps them quiet and subservient:

Do you think when the really talented people in the country get to work they get to work for us? Hell if they do! Do you think they don't know we 'ont make the effort? The writers don't write thinkin' we can understand, nor the painters don't paint expecting us to be interested – that they don't . . . 'Blust', they say, 'the masses is too stupid for us to come down to them' . . . So you know who come along? The slop singers and the pop writers and the film makers and women's magazines and the Sunday papers and the picture strip love stories – that's who come along, and you don't have to make no effort for them . . . Anything's good enough for them 'cos they don't ask for no more!

Edward Bond, from an avowedly Marxist perspective, began to depict a national malaise in a repressive class system. His highly controversial *Saved* (1965) showed scenes of savage violence that were to prove unacceptable to the Lord Chamberlain, who banned the play. In one scene a gang of youths stone a baby in a pram to death, having previously abused it horribly. Bond does not explicitly condemn the youths but tries to show that the entire family of the baby are being slowly 'murdered', certainly dehumanised, by the deprivation of their lives. In the Preface he claimed:

> Clearly the stoning to death of a baby in a London park is a typical English understatement. Compared to the 'strategic' bombing of German towns it is a negligible atrocity, compared to the cultural and emotional deprivation of most of our children its consequences are insignificant.

Bond's *Saved* was presented in the year when the Vietnam War began, and his preoccupation with violence was linked to a general awareness that the world was in danger. In 1956, Britain had been involved in an aggressive débâcle against Egypt over the ownership of the Suez Canal and in the same year Hungary was invaded by Soviet forces intent on crushing a recalcitrant satellite. Bond further justified his need to confront violence in his Preface to *Lear*:

> I write about violence as naturally as Jane Austen wrote about manners. Violence shapes and obsesses our society, and if we do not stop being violent we have no future. People who do not want writers to write about violence want to stop them writing about us and

our time. It would be immoral not to write about violence.

Bond's plays were strongly supported by the Royal Court Theatre (and he was later performed by the Royal Shakespeare Company and the National Theatre), and they laid down a challenge as to what 'theatre' might be – because they were so far removed from the mild entertainment of the early 1950s. They inspired and paved the way for a younger generation of politically motivated writers who dominated the late 1960s and 1970s – notably David Hare, Howard Brenton, Trevor Griffiths and David Edgar.

Foreign Influences

In the 1950s the British theatre, traditionally fairly insular, began to take notice of developments in post-war European theatre. In 1955, Samuel Beckett's play *Waiting for Godot* was performed in London, and in the next year the East German playwright Bertolt Brecht's company, the Berliner Ensemble, visited London. Both offered a fundamental challenge to the cosy naturalism of most contemporary English drama. Both Brecht and Beckett, but in very different ways, offered a response to the horror and despair generated by the experience of the Second World War. Beckett's plays continued to be performed in Britain on a regular basis, and Brechtian influences were to become marked in the work of English 'political' dramatists.

Beckett was given the primary position in Martin Esslin's widely read book *The Theatre of the Absurd*, in which a number of European dramatists of the 1940s and

1950s are defined as reacting to the absence of reason, order and meaning in the human condition. Eugene Ionesco, the author of *The Bald Prima Donna* and *The Chairs*, defined 'the Absurd' as 'that which is devoid of purpose . . . Cut off from his religious, metaphysical and transcendent roots, man is lost; all his actions become senseless, absurd, useless' (*Esslin*, p. 23). This philosophical basis for the definition of 'absurd' derives from the French novelist and dramatist Albert Camus, who claimed, 'in a universe that is suddenly deprived of illusions and of light, man feels a stranger . . . This divorce between man and his life, the actor and his setting, truly constitutes the feeling of Absurdity.' Above all, the human condition is seen as existing in a world devoid of 'God'. The naturalistic form of theatre, with its emphasis on the familiar, was regarded as inappropriate to convey these insights, and a number of European dramatists – including, for example, Beckett, Ionesco, Adamov, Genet and Arrabal – devised new forms and images for the stage. In Beckett, all human action is pointless. *Waiting for Godot*, *Endgame* and *Happy Days* each shows characters physically trapped and subject to the one and only certainty, the passing of time. Hamm is blind and confined to a wheelchair, Winnie is buried to the neck in sand and Vladimir and Estragon are locked in a pattern of circular 'routines' which repeatedly end where they began. The effect can be comic when the two tramps/clowns perform together, but it is none the less pathetic:

ESTRAGON: Carry on.
VLADIMIR: No no, after you.
ESTRAGON: No no, you first.
VLADIMIR: I interrupted you.

ESTRAGON: On the contrary.
They glare at each other angrily.
VLADIMIR: Ceremonious ape!
ESTRAGON: Punctilious pig!
VLADIMIR: Finish your phrase, I tell you!
ESTRAGON: Finish your own!
Silence. They draw closer, halt.
VLADIMIR: Moron!
ESTRAGON: That's the idea, let's abuse each other.
They turn, move apart, turn again and face each other.
VLADIMIR: Moron!
ESTRAGON: Vermin!
VLADIMIR: Abortion!
ESTRAGON: Morpion!
VLADIMIR: Sewer-rat!
ESTRAGON: Curate!
VLADIMIR: Cretin!
ESTRAGON: (*with finality*) Crritic!
VLADIMIR: Oh!
He wilts, vanquished, and turns away.
ESTRAGON: Now let's make up.
VLADIMIR: Gogo!
ESTRAGON: Didi!

Brecht could hardly be more different. His Marxist philosophy elevated human reason as the hope for the future. He developed an 'Epic Theatre', and in plays such as *Mother Courage*, *The Life of Galileo* and *The Good Woman of Setzuan* he progressed from the obvious political didacticism of his early work to parables where human inadequacy is fully recognised and the need for change is clearly shown. The universe is still 'Godless' and the nature of reality has a very 'material' base, but it is within man's power to effect change. Brecht's audience is credited with reason and intelligence and is encouraged to change its thinking. What was strikingly impressive and most influential about the visit of the Berliner Ensemble to London in 1956, however, was the palpable artistic value of a permanent acting ensemble. Brecht worked with his company over a period of years and evolved a style in which acting and design were perfectly matched to his plays, and where every part, however small, was recognised as vital to the whole. Soon after Brecht's company visited London the notion of 'the company' began to dominate the English theatre.

Pinter and the New Writing

It should be clear from this brief survey of developments in the British theatre during the 1950s and 1960s that Pinter's arrival as a dramatist coincided with a sudden proliferation of new work and new ideas about the theatre. Inevitably, dramatists appearing at the same time began to be linked or grouped according to their style or content, and so was Harold Pinter. The unspecified 'menace' associated with the world outside, the mixing of comedy and serious stress, the lack of verification about the past, and the seeming 'absurdity' of some of his dramatic situations all allowed for Pinter to be included as an 'Absurdist' by Esslin in his book on the subject. Furthermore, Pinter is an avowed admirer of the work of Samuel Beckett, whose sparse dialogue and bleak vision are seen to be influential in Pinter's plays. However, Esslin always recognised the extent to which Pinter's plays can be regarded 'realistically', and Pinter could easily be linked with the new writers who were concerned to deal seriously with the 'working class'. So all the characters in *The Caretaker*, for example, can be seen to be victims of an uncaring society: Aston the victim of institutionalised brutality, Davies a suffering social reject, and Mick an isolated and aimless neurotic. Though never associated in his plays with 'party politics', there is unquestionably a 'political' dimension to *The Birthday Party*. Also there is a strong vein of violence in many Pinter plays which link them with the rhetorical violence of Osborne and the physical violence of Bond. All this linking and connecting of Pinter with other writers is, however, academic grist to the mill. He has always denied the kind of 'commitment' that linked 'social' dramatists associated with the Royal Court Theatre. He was never part of any group. In actual fact Pinter has acknowledged that recognised forms of drama, such as comedy, tragedy or farce, were breaking down at this period of time and becoming irrelevant as terms of definition (see *Plays Two*, p. xi). Most significantly, the title of Pinter's Introduction to *Plays Two* is 'Writing for Myself', and he is adamant that 'Firstly and finally, and all along the line, you write because there's something you *want* to write, *have* to write. For yourself' (*Plays Two*, p. ix). Pinter's unique style of poetic realism made him a dramatist set apart, *sui generis*, and this is what he has remained.

The Birthday Party

Synopsis

ACT ONE The play is set in the living room of a house in an English seaside town. Act One occurs during a morning in summer. Petey enters with a newspaper, sits at the table and begins to read. Meg serves his breakfast and questions him about the paper and about 'that boy' Stanley, who has not yet got up. Meg and Petey are in their sixties. Petey says that two men have asked him if they can stay for a couple of nights. Meg replies that she has a room available, claiming that theirs is a very good boarding house. Meg exits to wake Stanley and we hear shouts from him and wild laughter from Meg. She returns 'panting and arranging her hair' and Stanley enters, unshaven, in his pyjama jacket. He is a man in his late thirties. Meg serves his breakfast. Petey leaves, returning to his work as a deckchair attendant. Stanley teases and taunts Meg for her inadequacies both as a cook and a wife to Petey. She fusses around Stanley with annoying intimacy until he is forced to leave in disgust. When he returns Meg announces that she is expecting two visitors. Stanley is very alarmed at this prospect. He tells Meg that he is considering a job abroad as a pianist, and describes how he had once given a concert that was a great success but that his career was cut short by unscrupulous people. He then frightens Meg with a story about how people are coming that day in a van with a wheelbarrow to take

34

somebody away. Lulu – a neighbour, in her twenties – enters, carrying a parcel. She complains about Stanley's scruffy appearance but nevertheless invites him out for a walk. When Stanley declines she describes him as 'a bit of a washout', and leaves. Stanley is washing his face in the kitchen when Goldberg and McCann enter. McCann is on edge but Goldberg appears full of confidence and begins to reminisce enthusiastically about his early life. The two have apparently come to do 'a job', and Goldberg is clearly in charge; the job, which worries McCann, is not explained. When Meg returns she is warmly greeted by Goldberg. She tells him that Stanley is her only guest and that today is his birthday. Goldberg proposes a party for Stanley at nine o'clock that evening. He and McCann exit to their room upstairs. Stanley is very disturbed by the arrival of the two strangers but Meg tries to cheer him up by mentioning the party. She gives him a present: the parcel brought in by Lulu. It is a toy drum. Stanley puts it round his neck and marches round the table beating it. He stops in front of Meg, 'his face and the drumbeat now savage and possessed'.

ACT TWO It is evening and McCann is sitting at the table tearing a sheet of newspaper into five equal strips. Stanley enters and McCann holds him in conversation. Stanley is fearful of Goldberg and tries unsuccessfully to ingratiate himself with McCann. Goldberg enters with Petey, again talking of 'the good old days'. Petey leaves for his weekly game of chess and McCann goes with him to collect bottles for the party. Alone with Goldberg, Stanley insists that the two men have come to the wrong house and must leave. When McCann returns Stanley is subjected to a ferocious cross-examination. He is accused of a great

catalogue of supposed offences against the family, religion
and the state. Stanley reacts violently against Goldberg
but is reduced to an inarticulate victim. Meg enters,
dressed for the party, carrying Stanley's drum. Stanley, in
silence, serves drinks for all and Meg proposes an
emotional toast to him on his birthday. Lulu enters and
is immediately impressed by Goldberg's fluency. They all
toast Stanley and the party begins, Lulu joining Goldberg
and Meg joining McCann, who sings an Irish song. Meg
wants a game and the group, organised by Goldberg,
play blind man's buff. When it is Stanley's turn to be
blindfolded, McCann ensures that he catches his foot in
the drum, which he drags behind him until he reaches
Meg. He begins to strangle her, but is restrained by
Goldberg and McCann before the stage is plunged into
darkness. McCann has a torch but it is knocked from his
hand and in the darkness Lulu is terrified at being touched
and faints. When the torch is found Stanley is discovered
bending over Lulu, who is spreadeagled across the table.
As Stanley begins to giggle, Goldberg and McCann
converge upon him.

ACT THREE Next morning Petey enters with a newspaper
and sits at the table. Meg, suffering from a hangover,
pours him a cup of tea. The situation mirrors the opening
of the play. Meg wants to wake Stanley, but Petey is
anxious for her to leave the house and do her shopping.
Meg is frightened by the big car parked outside the house
but is relieved to hear that it belongs to Goldberg. When
Goldberg enters he is noticeably less confident. He
explains to Petey that Stanley has suffered a nervous
breakdown. Petey thinks he needs a doctor but Goldberg
insists that he will look after Stanley by taking him to

Monty, who has 'qualifications'. When McCann enters he is very disturbed and wants to 'get it over and go'. Goldberg begins to collapse and seeks McCann's help. Lulu enters and is aggrieved at how Goldberg has abused her. McCann demands that she 'confess' but she becomes more angry at Goldberg's indifference. Stanley enters and appears completely changed – he is clean-shaven and dressed in a dark well-cut suit and white collar. Goldberg and McCann 'begin to woo him, gently and with relish', in a sequence that parallels the interrogation of Act Two. They promise Stanley a future of success where they will provide 'proper care and treatment'. Stanley can reply only with inarticulate grunts and sounds from his throat. They take Stanley away, ignoring Petey's plea that they leave him. When Meg returns she remembers the 'lovely' party where she was 'the belle of the ball'.

The Play

By arriving from nowhere and taking Stanley away, Goldberg and McCann echo a hugely pervasive idea in Western culture: if you don't behave, somebody will come and get you. This is the original bogeyman story, used to frighten children, made dramatically real. However, Stanley's offence is never made clear and so his nightmare experience during the play becomes a metaphor for the fear that anyone might have of offending society at large.

The individual and society

The idea of some crime or misdeed in the past coming to haunt the present is very old in drama. It is the subject of *Oedipus Rex*, of Ibsen's *Ghosts*, of Miller's *All My Sons*, O'Neill's *Long Day's Journey Into Night*, and Priestley's

An Inspector Calls. As Arthur Miller has explained, plays such as these deal with 'chickens coming home to roost' and the result is often tragic. An element of retribution or justice, even revenge, lies behind the action. Certainly there is no escape. The theme is reflected poignantly in Hemingway's story *The Killers*, where two unknown hitmen arrive in a small town and their victim knows there is nowhere else to go. (Stanley says to Lulu, 'There's nowhere to go.')

In these instances, however, the original misdeed is tangible and the guilt is acknowledged. In *The Birthday Party* we don't know for certain what Stanley has done, and he puts up what resistance he can against the two intruders who 'demand justice' (p. 91). Clearly Goldberg and McCann have come to get Stanley for some reason and the play, inevitably, invites us to consider what he has done to deserve this assault. The sheer range of accusations levelled at Stanley during the interrogation in Act Two, from the particular to the absurd, widens the issue. Instead of the tragic figure confronted by his mistake, Stanley seems more of a persecuted victim, and as such he relates to another theme of modern literature which concerns the individual and society, and the individual's sense of guilt. A most influential work on this subject is Franz Kafka's *The Trial* (1925), which begins, 'Somebody must have made a false accusation against Joseph K., for he was arrested one morning without having done anything wrong.'

Pinter has said, 'I read *The Trial* when I was a lad of eighteen, in 1948. It's been with me ever since. I don't think anyone who reads *the Trial* – it ever leaves them.' He was to adapt the novel for a film, made in 1990. Although easily confused with the context and culture of an Eastern

European communist state during the Cold War, *The Trial* is actually set in the world of the Austro-Hungarian Empire at the end of the last century. Joseph K. is the victim of a vast bureaucracy. Brought before an examining magistrate, Joseph exposes the proceedings:

> There is no doubt that behind all the utterances of this court, and therefore behind my arrest and examination, there stands a great organisation. An organisation which not only employs corrupt warders and fatuous supervisors and examining magistrates, of whom the best that can be said is that they are humble officials, but also supports a judiciary of the highest rank with its inevitable vast retinue of servants, secretaries, police officers and other assistants, perhaps even executioners – I don't shrink from the word. And the purpose of this great organisation, gentlemen? To arrest innocent persons and start proceedings against them . . . (p. 36)

It is possible to see similarities between the lot of Stanley and Joseph K. Both attract two strangers to arrest them on their birthday (Joseph is thirty). The arresting officers in each case employ language games, and have unspecified superiors who would seem to represent 'the establishment'. Both Stanley and Joseph K. suffer from paranoia, implying that in both cases the law is drawn remorselessly towards guilt.

During the twentieth century the individual has become increasingly alienated and distanced from the centres of power. Arthur Miller has cited many examples of how this power has operated against the individual in the modern world, but senses that it is an age-old theme: 'this placing holiness on the government, government being a holy entity, and the individual being an unholy one . . .' At

its worst we have instances of Hitler, Stalin, McCarthy –
and their brutality reflected in works such as Miller's own
The Crucible or Orwell's *1984*. In *The Birthday Party*
there is no indication that Stanley has been a danger to the
state, or that he has threatened it in any way. His offence
is not of a directly political nature. He does seem,
nevertheless, to have offended against the 'holy entity' –
the unspecified authorities whose agents are Goldberg and
McCann. Here the individual is crushed below the weight
of social expectations, rather than specific tyranny. As in
the case of Willy Loman in *Death of a Salesman*, who
cannot live up to the American dream of material success,
Stanley is never fully aware of what he has done wrong.

Harold Hobson realised the seriousness underlying the
comic elements in *The Birthday Party* when he reviewed
the first production:

> Mr Pinter has got hold of a primary fact of existence.
> We live on the verge of disaster. One sunny afternoon
> . . . a hydrogen bomb may explode. That is one sort of
> threat. But Mr Pinter's is of a subtler sort. It breathes in
> the air. It cannot be seen, but it enters the room every
> time the door is opened. There is something in your
> past – it does not matter what – which will catch up
> with you. Though you go to the uttermost parts of the
> earth and hide yourself in the most obscure lodgings in
> the least popular of towns, one day there is a possibility
> that two men will appear. They will be looking for you,
> and you cannot get away. And someone will be looking
> for *them* too. There is terror everywhere. (*Sunday
> Times*, 25 May 1958)

The play as metaphor

Pinter is most reluctant to explain his plays, but he has been quite explicit about *The Birthday Party*. In a letter to the original director, Peter Wood (not published until 1981) he writes: 'We've agreed; the hierarchy, the Establishment, the arbiters, the socio-religious monsters arrive to effect alteration and censure upon a member of the club who has discarded responsibility . . . towards himself and others.' And in an interview with Mel Gussow he let slip, 'Between you and me, the play showed how the bastards . . . how religious forces ruin our lives.' So the allegorical dimension is not in dispute. This play, like *The Hothouse* and *The Dumb Waiter*, is partly a metaphor.

However, while this goes some way towards explaining the function of Goldberg and McCann, who represent the Judaeo-Christian tradition in Western civilisation that demands conformity towards family, state and church, it doesn't take us far with Stanley. What has he done to deserve the nightmare that he suffers during the play? To begin with, he appears to be unkempt, lazy and self-indulgent, but does that merit torture and mental breakdown? Part of the suspense that holds our attention throughout the play is due precisely to the indeterminate nature of Stanley's past. We never learn what he might actually have done to attract the attentions of Goldberg and McCann. There are, however, some tantalising connections which operate like poetic imagery linking Stanley and Goldberg. For example, Goldberg talks of his Uncle Barney who 'had a house just outside Basingstoke' (p. 42). Later, when Stanley is pleading to McCann, he says, 'I've explained to you, damn you, that all those years I lived in Basingstoke I never stepped outside the door'

(p. 72). Similarly it is impossible to miss the connection between this:

> STANLEY: Ever been anywhere near Maidenhead?
> MCCANN: No.
> STANLEY: There's a Fuller's tea shop. I used to have my tea there.
> MCCANN: I don't know it.
> STANLEY: And a Boots Library. I seem to connect you with the High Street. (pp. 65–6)

and Goldberg's reference sometime later: 'A little Austin, tea in Fuller's, a library book from Boots, and I'm satisfied' (p. 102). These cross-references cannot be mere coincidences. They implicitly connect Stanley with Goldberg and McCann in the past. But not precisely so. The effect is surreal. It contributes to how Goldberg and McCann may be regarded imaginatively as figments of Stanley's subconscious guilt *as well as* stage people. Their arrival is inevitable, as Goldberg admits – 'If we hadn't come today we'd have come tomorrow' (p. 52). In his poem *A View of the Party* (1958), which comments directly and helpfully on the action of the play, Pinter writes:

> The thought that Goldberg was
> A man to dread and know
> Jarred Stanley in the blood
> When, still, he heard his name.
> [. . .]
> For Stanley had no home.
> Only where Goldberg was (*Casebook*, pp. 83–4)

This suggests quite strongly that Goldberg is part of Stanley's consciousness and, indeed, conscience. In this respect he fulfils a dramatic role not unlike Ariel in Shakespeare's *The Tempest*. Ariel is a character played by an actor, a distinct presence with his own words, but he can be regarded as a part of Prospero's consciousness:

> PROSPERO: Come with a thought. I thank thee. Ariel: come.
> *Enter* ARIEL
> ARIEL: Thy thoughts I cleave to. What's thy pleasure?
> (IV. i. 164–5)

Goldberg is a fictional stage character, realised by an actor – a real presence in the room – but he is also symbolic. Or he might be. As Katherine Worth suggests, 'Pinter brilliantly conveys the suggestion that the inquisitors are unreal beings, a projection of Stanley's obscure dread, without quite destroying the possibility of their being taken as real; this is what makes them so alarming' (*Casebook*, p. 37). Certainly their interrogation of Stanley in Act Two and their reconstruction of him in Act Three show them to be agents of an 'establishment', but their own inner fears are also exposed and this keeps them in the realm of naturalism.

Martin Esslin convincingly argues that 'A play like *The Birthday Party* can only be understood as a complex poetic image. Such an image exists, simultaneously, on a multitude of levels. A complex pattern of association and allusion is assembled to express a complex emotional state; what the poet tries to communicate by such an image is, ultimately, the totality of his own existential anxiety' (*Esslin*, pp. 70–1). Thus Stanley is guilty of being Stanley. His fears concern the world outside, which makes immeasurable demands on him (the individual) from the kinds of directions which he chooses not to fulfil.

Questions of identity

A disturbing aspect of *The Birthday Party*, which confused the first critics and audiences of the play, are the unanswered questions concerning the background of the characters. However, this uncertainty about 'identity' is crucial. It relates to all the characters. Stanley's experience of guilt is reflected in his paranoid response on hearing of the 'two visitors'. It seems clear that he has run away from something and has sought refuge with Meg and Petey. Here he does nothing at all but exist. The one clear fact about his past would seem to be that he once played the piano – Meg has seen him doing so, and he talks of it himself. But he has given up on that, and the details of his history are so vague that it seems unpromising to pursue an interpretation of the play that makes Stanley a representative 'artist' in society. The fact is, as Pinter has said, that Stanley has 'discarded responsibility towards himself and others' (*Casebook*, p. 82). He has opted out, and society takes revenge.

The question of Stanley's guilt, however, and the variety of accusations levelled at him, and the promises made to him at the end, all raise the fundamental issue of 'identity' which preoccupies Pinter in this play as in many others. To define one's identity simply as 'the fact of being who or what one is' has never satisfied Pinter. His whole theory of the way we use language is based on his belief that we do not wish to be 'known' and we don't wish to know other people. Furthermore, he isn't at all confident that we can even know 'who we are'. In a programme note for the Royal Court Theatre's production of *The Room* and *The Dumb Waiter* (1960) Pinter wrote:

The desire for verification is understandable but cannot always be satisfied. There are no hard distinctions between what is real and what is unreal, nor between what is true and what is false. The thing is not necessarily either true or false; it can be both true and false. The assumption that to verify what has happened and what is happening presents few problems I take to be inaccurate. A character on the stage who can present no convincing argument or information as to his past experience, his present behaviour or his aspirations, nor give a comprehensive analysis of his motives, is as legitimate and as worthy of attention as one who, alarmingly, can do all these things. The more acute the experience the less articulate its expression.

This lengthy quotation applies very closely to *The Birthday Party*. Take, for example, the last lines of the play, when Meg insists that she was 'the belle of the ball':

MEG: Oh, it's true. I was.
Pause.
I know I was. (p. 164)

Her conviction may not accord with what we have actually seen. It is true – to her – and not true. But then Meg does not perceive the world very clearly. Early in the play Stanley relates the story of his successful piano concert – *to himself* (stage direction) – but Meg is listening (p. 31). The story is not very detailed, but when Meg recalls it to Goldberg, ten minutes later, she produces a completely garbled and incorrect version:

MEG: (*falteringly*) In . . . a big hall. His father gave him champagne. But then they locked the place up and he couldn't get out. The caretaker had gone home. So he

45

had to wait until the morning before he could get
out . . . (p. 50)

Not only does she misrepresent the details (Stanley says
that his father did not attend the concert), but she has
delivered to Goldberg information which *he* may take as
fact and so Goldberg's knowledge of 'what is true' begins
from a wrong premise. The confusion about the facts of
the past is further compounded because we have no way
of knowing whether Stanley was telling the truth in the
first place. As Pinter has said, 'we are faced with the
immense difficulty, if not the impossibility, of verifying
the past. I don't mean merely years ago, but yesterday,
this morning' (*V.V.*, p. 17).

There are many details of the past mentioned in *The
Birthday Party* which bring an element of confusion to the
present and cause doubts about the identities of characters
on stage. Goldberg, in particular, is constantly referring
to his past as a time of 'golden days' ('What days', 'What a
life'), solid and reliable family suport ('I had a wife. What
a wife.'), complete happiness and success:

And that's why I've reached my position, McCann.
Because I've always been as fit as a fiddle. My motto.
Work hard and play hard. Not a day's illness.

This is so much a part of his self-presentation that the
whole edifice begins to smack of wishful thinking, as if
Goldberg were trying to convince himself. He may boast
that 'every single one of my senses is at its peak', but his
confidence does not last and he eventually loses his
panache. In Act Three he comes close to desperation – 'I
don't know why, but I feel knocked out. I feel a bit . . . It's
uncommon for me.' The past is made the more confusing

by Goldberg's array of names – McCann calls him Nat, but in the past he was called Simey and also Benny. McCann is also referred to as Seamus and Dermot, and he, too, is a complex personality and his 'identity' is uncertain. He is riddled with fanatical prejudices, but sentimental when drunk; he behaves like a gangster, but we learn, 'He's only been unfrocked six months'; he exudes menace but is also insecure:

> GOLDBERG: McCann, what are you so nervous about? Pull yourself together. Everywhere you go these days it's like a funeral. (p. 43)

Even Lulu, who might appear an uncomplicated character and a girl of little depth, has a past which affects her present behaviour – but it is not given any detailed exploration. She is drawn to Goldberg partly by this undisclosed history – 'Do you think you knew me when I was a little girl?' she says, and 'You're the dead image of the first man I ever loved.'

At the centre of the action is Stanley and the details of his identity are the most tantalising. The play simply does not reveal why he has chosen to live with Meg and Petey or what he might have done to bring Goldberg and McCann down to get him. The play is disturbing because this kind of detail would normally be disclosed. At the end of a thriller everything is usually revealed. The guilty party is exposed. In the case of Stanley what we see is all we know. Stanley is an exceptionally unremarkable central figure, and this is a vital aspect of the play. He is not permitted to be himself, whatever and whoever he is. Goldberg and McCann effectively destroy his identity and transform him into the visual representative of respectable society – *dressed in a dark well-cut suit and white collar*' (p. 151). In appearance he is completely altered, but in fact he has become dehumanised because he has lost the definitive mark of identity – the power of human speech.

Characters

GOLDBERG AND MCCANN The two intruders, Goldberg and McCann, arrive together and form one of the most famous double-acts in modern drama. As with Stoppard's Rosencrantz and Guildenstern (*Rosencrantz and Guildenstern Are Dead*) and Beckett's Estragon and Vladimir (*Waiting For Godot*) or Ham and Clov (*Endgame*), they are a dramatic duo who operate in tandem. Immediately recognisable as a (cockney) Jew and an Irishman, and constantly drawing attention to their racial characteristics, they might be relegated to the status of purely comic figures. In fact the music-hall double-act is always cited as the basis of their stage presence. Also their language and references are always very close to parody. However, Pinter has made two references to them which indicate that they are more interesting.

Firstly, as representatives of traditional values, Pinter is merciless about them – 'Dying, rotting, scabrous, the decayed spiders, the flower of our society. They know their way around. Our mentors. Our ancestry. Them. Fuck 'em' (*V.V.*, p. 10). However, he was later to admit, 'I suppose that Goldberg and McCann in *The Birthday Party* are regarded as an *evil pair*, but I'm very fond of them' (*Gussow*, p. 20). Obviously, he created them; and he has played Goldberg on stage and on film. But his enthusiasm is likely to derive from his recognition that they are marvellous parts to play because they are fully realised characters. They are also vulnerable characters – subject to and victims of their social background. Both are deeply insecure, and this becomes increasingly evident during the play. The two can easily be seen to be acting on behalf of the dark forces of social orthodoxy, and as such – which is very unusual in Pinter – fulfilling a symbolic role in the play. This has been considered above, and is acknowledged by Pinter himself. However, an actor cannot get very far playing 'a symbol' (as will be considered further in relation to Ruth in *The Home-coming*). An actor begins with his 'character', and both Goldberg and McCann are vivid stage characters.

From their first entrance the two are sharply distinguished. Goldberg is in charge, relaxed, outgoing and full of confidence. McCann is nervous, uncertain and introverted. They make a compelling impact because of this difference and because although we are not certain about why they have come, neither is McCann. They are a heavyweight pair who bring with them an aura of suspense and menace, made all the more disturbing by Goldberg's cheerfulness. Pinter's poem 'A View of the Party' states:

> Nat Goldberg, who arrived
> With a smile on every face,
> Accompanied by McCann,
> Set a change upon the place.
>
> The thought that Goldberg was
> Sat in the centre of the room,
> A man of weight and time,
> To supervise the game.

> The thought that was McCann
> Walked in upon the feast,
> A man of skin and bone,
> With a green stain on his chest. (V.V., p. 136)

Their behaviour, their speech and their prejudices owe everything to their social background. Ironically, in this play two of the most oppressed, even persecuted, communities – the Irish and the Jews – become the tormentors.

STANLEY The problem that exists with regard to Stanley is that the play does not make explicit what exactly he has done to provoke the arrival of Goldberg and McCann. His behaviour on hearing of them, and his reaction when they arrive, both suggest guilt, but the guilt is undefined. This, of course, is the whole point of the play. The accusations that are levelled at him during the interrogation of Act Two become so bizarre that the situation moves into the surreal and what is shown is a mental breakdown caused by a horrific verbal assault by two overpowering bullies. It can't be argued that Stanley is a classic case study of 'paranoia' because that is a mental disorder marked by the *unjustified* belief that one is being persecuted. Stanley *is* persecuted by Goldberg and McCann and, by extension, the 'Monty' who sent them (and all that he might represent). This is what we are shown in the play and in performance. So, any interpretation of the play which sees the action as allegorical, and Goldberg and McCann an extension of Stanley's subconscious guilt, is not likely to impress the actor playing the part of Stanley. The character is filled with dread, as anybody would be in his position. Stanley, as he is, cannot be tolerated by the powers that exist who require something different, but these 'powers' are realised by two very unpleasant and very real opponents:

GOLDBERG: We'll make a man of you.
MCCANN: And a woman.
GOLDBERG: You'll be re-orientated.
MCCANN: You'll be rich.
GOLDBERG: You'll be adjusted.
MCCANN: You'll be our pride and joy.
GOLDBERG: You'll be a mensch.
MCCANN: You'll be a success
GOLDBERG: You'll be integrated. (pp. 156–7)

These promises are no more specific than the earlier accusations. Indeed they are meaningless. The intruders are intent on changing Stanley's identity, which they do. Stanley's final entrance, clean-shaven and dressed in a dark well-cut suit and white collar – in marked contrast to his earlier appearance – makes him look a figure of anonymous conformity. The evidence of the play, therefore, is that Stanley has offended not by committing a particular offence but by not conforming, and in Act One the characteristics of his non-conformity are shown.

Stanley is revealed as having retreated to a family home where he can indulge himself by doing nothing. Here he sleeps for as long as he likes (Meg to Petey: 'You say he stays in bed too much'), fails to dress or wash properly, and is looked after by an adoring, if simple-minded, mother-substitute. He can drink his cups of tea and smoke his cigarettes. It is not a prepossessing picture. Stanley is the opposite of a romantic hero; and even as an 'Everyman' figure he is a very run-down example. By any of the standards that society uses to define 'success' Stanley is a failure. If ever he was a competent pianist it is clear that he has now given up playing the piano. Lulu calls him a washout and the same term is used by Goldberg. The negative side of his character is underlined in the first part of the play. Nevertheless, despite all this, Pinter sees Stanley as a 'free' man. He is not answerable to anybody and he does nobody any harm. By 'opting-out' of traditional responsibilities (obligations, for example, to family, career and society) he is exercising his freedom. However, his earlier life would inevitably have left a weighty sense of what exactly he has chosen to do, with an accompanying sense of guilt. This guilt is manifest as soon as he hears of Goldberg and McCann, who arrive to impose society's revenge. Stanley puts up something of a fight to begin with:

> STANLEY: Let me – just make this clear. You don't bother me. To me, you're nothing but a dirty joke. But I have a responsibility towards the people in this house. They've been down here too long. They've lost their sense of smell. I haven't. And nobody's going to take advantage of them while I'm here. (pp. 77–8)

But he has no chance against their combined assault and he collapses, mentally, under their persecution. Stanley's behaviour during the climax of the birthday party, when he attacks Meg and appears to assault Lulu, gives rise to a variety of psychoanalytical interpretations of what has been repressed in Stanley's psyche, and what is now given full expression – the fear of the father (Goldberg is clearly a 'father-figure'), the love/hate resentment of the mother (Meg), and the love/hate resentment of adult sexuality (manifest in Lulu). Pinter has said that Stanley 'has lost any adult comprehension and reverts to a childhood malice and mischief, as his first shelter' (*V.V.*, p. 11). This is not to deny the force of the subconscious and the deep-rooted psychological motives which are beyond Stanley's control. The full details of the dreadful night that follows are left mysterious and awful. When Stanley reappears in the morning, newly dressed, he is in a catatonic state. He is wooed back into a world where he will be able to 'see straight' for the first time and promised all the supposed benefits of conformity. Stanley cannot speak but the sounds coming from his throat, and his concentrated shuddering body, suggest a last desperate rejection of what is happening to him.

In peformance, our reaction to Stanley is bound to depend on the actor, as Pinter is well aware: 'A great deal, it seems to me, will depend on the actor. If he copes with Stanley's loss of himself successfully I believe a certain amount of poignancy will emanate. Couldn't we all find ourselves in Stanley's position at any given moment?' (*V.V.*, p. 11). Clearly this was achieved by Richard Pearson, who, according to the *Observer*, played Stanley 'as the archetypal victim, the fat boy with glasses. He was idle, sweaty, suspicious, edgy and highly sympathetic. This was an intelligent man who looked stupid, partly out of self-defence.'

MEG AND PETEY The play begins and ends with Meg and Petey, who create a naturalistic environment for the action. Meg is interesting in so far as her progress through the play shows something of Pinter's attitude towards characterisation. He never treats her patronisingly, as Noël Coward might extract fun from a housemaid in a sophisticated house. It would be a strange production that did not find *some* humour in her early exchanges with

Petey and Stanley (boasting of her fried-bread breakfast, failing to recognise 'Lady Mary Splatt' from the newspaper, confusing the term 'succulent'), where her lack of intelligence is all too evident. But her limitations are not only exposed for amusement. She is instantly terrified by Stanley's threat of a wheelbarrow coming to take someone away. Always the totality of her personality is there for an actress to work on. Essentially she is a bundle of instincts and she has very little intelligence. The poet R. S. Thomas writes of *A Peasant* that 'There is something frightening in the vacancy of his mind' and this might apply to Meg. Stanley is adamant, when talking to McCann, that 'She's crazy. Round the bend', and 'That woman is mad' (p. 70). During the birthday party and under the influence of whisky, Meg reminisces, 'There was a night-light in my room, when I was a little girl.' She had a nanny, and

> My little room was pink . . . and my father was a very big doctor. That's why I never had any complaints. I was cared for, and I had little sisters and brothers in other rooms, all different colours. (p. 111)

The clues here of an institutional background hint at the possibility of her being an extremely backward child. But Pinter has followed the character seriously, and taken her beyond what is generally considered to be one of the initial images for the play – quoted in a letter written to a friend when Pinter was touring as an actor:

> I have filthy insane digs, a great bulging scrag of a woman with breasts rolling at her belly, an obscene household, cats, dogs, filth . . . deficient order in the upper fretwork. (*File on Pinter*, Methuen, 1993, p. 12)

This is hardly a fair description of Meg, who gains significantly from the gentle attention of Petey both at the beginning and end of the play. Meg's affection for Stanley is disturbing because he so clearly is not the little boy of her imagining and desire. Watching how Stanley keeps her at a distance it is improbable that she has had any sexual relations with him, despite the innuendo 'I've had some lovely afternoons in that room.' The mother–son relationship is much more compelling. Her attentions are insufferable and irritating, but her affection is genuine. The most disturbing feature of her presence in the play, however, is her close involvement with all the other characters and her complete inability to understand what is going on. Pinter recognises how far individuals are isolated, even when living in close proximity with others. Her relationship with Petey has become one of habit. Petey is tolerant, observant, but leads a life of quiet simplicity – attending deckchairs, reading the paper, playing a weekly game of chess and working in his garden. At first he is taken in by Goldberg and McCann, but in Act Three he causes Goldberg, in particular, some fright when he holds his ground ('Well, I think I'll see how my peas are getting on, in the meantime'). Finally, and understandably, he wants no trouble. But his last words to Stanley have become a personal mantra, by his own admission, for Pinter himself:

PETEY: (*broken*) Stan, don't let them tell you what to do! (p. 161)

LULU Lulu is not a complicated character, which reflects her function in the play. Her lack of sophistication and her naivety help to keep the action in a real world.

55

Probably bored to death, she is prepared to go for a walk with Stanley, which he resists. The main purpose of her scene with him in Act One is to expose the extent of his slovenliness and his state of desperation. He wants to escape but he dare not. Lulu simply sees what is in front of her, knowing nothing of Goldberg and McCann, and sums Stanley up – 'You're a bit of a washout, aren't you.' Her relationship with Goldberg in Acts Two and Three helps to keep him a character in a naturalistic world. He seduces her with consummate ease, because, as he says, 'You wanted me to do it.' During the birthday party she is completely taken in by Goldberg's grotesque eloquence and offers herself to 'the older man' quite willingly. In the morning her outraged response to his rejection is funny because it is couched in the most banal of clichés – 'You made use of me by cunning when my defences were down' . . . 'You didn't appreciate me for myself.'

Dramatic Structure

The Birthday Party is a conventional three-act play, with each act moving towards a powerful curtain-line. Act One concerns the arrival of Goldberg and McCann and Stanley's evident fear of them; Act Two concerns the breakdown of Stanley and the birthday party; Act Three shows Goldberg and McCann badly affected by the night's events and their removal of Stanley despite Petey's meagre efforts to protect him. All this takes place in a play-world that is clearly defined as real in a naturalistic sense.

The stage set reflects a living room of a real house, with three doors, a kitchen hatch, table and chairs. The coming and going of characters on this stage is carefully structured to ensure that everything is plausible. A good deal of stage business and many references, often banal in their ordinariness, help to keep the action fixed in an actual environment. A list of stage properties would emphasise this. Petey reads a newspaper. We are given cornflakes, fried bread and tea. We see Meg darning socks, dusting and going shopping (later to be seen emptying her bag). Lulu 'powders her nose' from a compact. Stanley smokes cigarettes. Goldberg and McCann arrive with suitcases. Whisky is brought in for the party. A torch is produced when the lights are put out. There is an equally strong sense of an outside world – with shops close by, a pub that sells draught Guinness and the beach where Petey works as a deckchair attendant. We know we are in a seaside town, probably on the south coast, not too far from London. Basingstoke and Maidenhead, southern towns, are evoked; and so is London – in both Goldberg and Stanley's reminiscences.

It is important to appreciate the solidity and actuality of this world, which is so carefully structured, because of what goes on within it. The action of the characters and their behaviour towards each other take on a heightened significance largely because the stylised language and bizarre events are placed in a real world. There are some very 'theatrical', disturbing moments in the play, but they do emerge logically from the preceding events. For example, in Act One, just as Stanley has brought Meg to a peak of terror by the threat of someone coming with a wheelbarrow, there is a stage direction – '*A sudden knock on the front door*' (p. 34). It is, in fact, Lulu dropping round a parcel ordered by Meg. In Act Two, at the height of Stanley's interrogation when there is a real threat of actual physical violence, there is another stage direction – '*A loud drumbeat off left, descending the stairs*' (p. 95). It is Meg arriving for the party, carrying sticks and a drum. The shocking and apparently melodramatic off-stage sounds are not arbitrary but a part of the ongoing action.

The logical progression of the action, as characters are shown to be affected by their relationships with each other, takes on an almost surreal dimension because of the dichotomy between stage naturalism and stylised dialogue. The play is structured around a series of confrontations, mostly dualogues, which in their cumulative effect pose disturbing insights into the way people behave. The 'reality' of the individual psyche, of personal identity, is shown to be a fragile entity and this is the more disturbing because of the banality of the setting. What people 'know' of the world is uncertain. There are a number of obvious mysteries which are never fully explained, such as what exactly Stanley has done to cause the arrival of Goldberg, and who the Monty to whom he is taken is. However the chasm that exists between people, their inability or refusal to disclose themselves fully and the secrecy of their inner lives become major subjects of the play.

The first two acts end at a moment of disturbing climax, and the play ends with what is an equally disturbing anti-climax showing that Meg – despite the horrors of the evening – 'saw nothing done'. The climactic centre of the play, following on from the interrogation and breakdown of Stanley, is the birthday party, stage-managed by Goldberg, which is a grotesque parody of what a party – a social celebration – should be. There is a toast (proposed in all innocence by Meg), speech-making, drinking, songs and party games, but all combining to create a ghastly nightmare for the chief celebrant, Stanley. The group pair off, with Goldberg taking his chance with Lulu while Meg and McCann reminisce morbidly under the influence of alcohol. Stanley remains silent and isolated throughout until he is forced into the game of blind man's buff, is tricked into breaking the drum and has his spectacles snapped by McCann. The complex emotions that are displayed by the variously unknowing party-goers are juxtaposed with what is a sustained torture of Stanley, who finally cracks and attacks the women. The tension and atmosphere of the scene is enhanced by the lighting changes – both exterior and interior (involving the use of McCann's torch) – which move the action into the realm of the macabre.

Language

The distance that exists between people, even people living in close proximity, can be explored by contrasting the language of the various dualogues in the play and how they convey differing linguistic strategies. Most often there is a subtextual level of hidden knowledge which motivates the dialogue, so that characters are not so much engaged in 'conversation' as in covering up their deepest worries, or transferring their fears onto others. Stanley is at the centre of all the action and dialogue.

PETEY AND MEG It is possible to regard Meg as something of a touchstone when language strategies are employed – because she tells the truth as she sees it. Hardly anybody else does. It is easy to dismiss Meg as fundamentally stupid, and there is a danger of playing her simply for laughs because of her idiotic responses, but she is a fully realised character and her relationship with Petey is genuine. The action of the play is sandwiched between two scenes of Meg and Petey at breakfast in their living room, and this ritual establishes a normality against which the intervening proceedings are shown to be dreadful. The relationship has been so long-standing that a pattern is established. Petey has come to accept Meg's limitations. Perhaps once they did keep a guest-house, perhaps Meg could once read for herself; now Petey is resigned to living with Meg and not listening to her. Their dialogue is inconsequential, stylised in its repetition, but very revealing of character. Meg has no mind, and Petey is wholly tolerant:

MEG: What time did you go out this morning, Petey?
PETEY: Same time as usual.
MEG: Was it dark?
PETEY: No, it was light.
MEG: (*beginning to darn*) But sometimes you go out in the morning and it's dark.
PETEY: That's in the winter.
MEG: Oh, in winter.
PETEY: Yes, it gets light later in winter.
MEG: Oh. (pp. 4–5)

The stylisation of their dialogue makes us listen more carefully, but it is not intended purely for our amusement. Despite the obvious repetition and play on 'up' and 'down' in the following exchange, Meg is focused entirely on the absent Stanley – whose entrance is being prepared for:

MEG: Is Stanley up yet?
PETEY: I don't know. Is he?
MEG: I don't know. I haven't seen him down yet.

PETEY: Well then, he can't be up.

MEG: Haven't you seen him down?

PETEY: I've only just come in.

MEG: He must be still asleep. (pp. 3–4)

When Petey mentions the two men wanting a room there is a solicitude in his questioning Meg, as if he had every reason to doubt that a room would be ready. Meg's cooking would suggest that she isn't used to visitors:

PETEY: They might turn up today. Can you do it?

MEG: Oh, I've got that lovely room they can have.

PETEY: You've got a room ready?

MEG: I've got the room with the armchair all ready for visitors.

PETEY: You're sure?

MEG: Yes, that'll be all right then, if they come today.

PETEY: Good. (p. 9)

Petey's gentle resignation and concern is in marked contrast to that of Goldberg when he first meets Meg. Here an actor is given a wonderful opportunity, with the simplest vocabulary, to exude the grossest hypocrisy:

MEG: Very pleased to meet you.

They shake hands.

GOLDBERG: We're pleased to meet you, too.

MEG: That's very nice.

GOLDBERG: You're right. How often do you meet someone it's a pleasure to meet?

MCCANN: Never.

GOLDBERG: But today it's different. How are you keeping, Mrs Boles?

MEG: Oh, very well, thank you.

GOLDBERG: Yes? Really?

MEG: Oh, yes, really.
GOLDBERG: I'm glad. (pp. 47–8)

Meg's naivety allows Goldberg to set her up continually with the most outrageous flattery ('Madam, you'll look like a tulip' . . . 'Walk up the boulevard. Let's have a look at you. What a carriage. What's your opinion McCann? Like a Countess, nothing less'). There is obvious comedy in this but a distinct hollowness, as Goldberg has revealed the full extent of his violence during the interrogation of Stanley. There is a stunning irony too in Goldberg's forcing Meg into proposing a birthday toast to Stanley, because in the midst of a protracted torture session, of which she is completely unaware, she speaks the most honest lines in the play – 'Well, I could cry because I'm so happy, having him here and not gone away, on his birthday, and there isn't anything I wouldn't do for him, and all you good people here tonight . . . (*she sobs*)' (p. 100). In contrast to Meg's unknowing but instinctive responses the other characters emerge as calculating.

The closing exchange between Meg and Petey (pp. 161–8), which echoes the first scene, carries none of the comedy derived earlier from our recognition of the quirks of meaningless, mindless chatter. After the removal of Stanley there is an even wider and more immediate separation between Meg and Petey. He knows that Stanley has been taken away, but doesn't tell Meg. She has no idea of what has happened to Stanley, and her memory of 'a lovely party last night' with herself as 'the belle of the ball' is a personal fantasy. Her last line – 'I know I was' is the final statement of how an individual perception of reality can be both true and false.

MEG AND STANLEY The relationship between Meg and Stanley early in Act One introduces the element of conflict in dialogue, which the play is going to develop into scenes of desperate self-defence by Stanley. Here the exchanges are mainly comic because of the difference in awareness between Stanley and Meg. At first Stanley has the advantage over Meg because he knows how much she wants him to be pleased with her – so he can tease her at will:

STANLEY: You're a bad wife.
MEG: I'm not. Who said I am?
STANLEY: Not to make your husband a cup of tea. Terrible.
MEG: He knows I'm not a bad wife.
STANLEY: Giving him sour milk instead.
MEG: It wasn't sour.
STANLEY: Disgraceful. (p. 17)

But there is an edge to the relationship because of Meg's maternal instincts being applied to an adult. Stanley can indulge himself, and use Meg, but he is irritated and disgusted by her physicality. He can keep her at a distance with the word 'succulent' (pp. 18–19), but his child-like frustrations eventually explode – 'Look, why don't you get this place cleared up! . . . I need a new room!' (p. 22).

The relationship undergoes a permanent change once Stanley learns of the two visitors. It is he who is now threatened. Hitherto he could control Meg with the threat of leaving; now Stanley's mind is wholly preoccupied with his danger, and this is also reflected in his dialogue with Meg. Under the threat to his fragile security, he begins to assert himself: 'Tell me, Mrs Boles, when you address yourself to me, do you ever ask yourself . . .' (p. 28); and when he turns to verbal bluster and reminiscence Meg is completely lost – 'STANLEY: I've . . . er . . . I've been offered a job, as a matter of fact. / MEG: What?' (p. 29). The knowledge of the 'two gentlemen' provides the subtext which completely separates Meg and Stanley. For Meg they mean nothing, for Stanley everything. Because the characters have been well established, Stanley's threatening Meg with a wheelbarrow in a van produces real fear. It may be nonsense, and the audience have no knowledge of what scares Stanley, but the dialogue is psychologically understandable.

STANLEY AND LULU The brief scene between Stanley and Lulu (pp. 36–40) is also dominated by the subtext – Stanley's fear of the strangers and his accompanying sense of guilt. Now it is Lulu's turn to dominate and Stanley's to retreat. She is perfectly ingenuous in her assessment of Stanley – she tells him what she sees: an unclean, unshaven, half-dressed 'washout', who refuses the reasonable offer of a walk outdoors. Stanley is completely exposed and his defensive tactic of weak jokes ('I always stand on the table when she sweeps the floor') is pathetic. However, the full extent of Stanley's ineptitude has a tragic dimension. He is simply incapable of doing anything to avoid catastrophe ('There's nowhere to go') and Lulu, like Meg, is uncomprehending of Stanley's predicament.

GOLDBERG AND MCCANN The entrance of Goldberg and McCann (p. 40) is double-edged in its effect. McCann's nervousness about 'the job' they have come to do continues the sense of disturbing menace and mystery, but Goldberg's expansive presence brings a comic dimension. The two – the Irishman and the Jew – provide a comic contrast and their dialogue is occasionally reminiscent of music-hall patter, which should not be lost on an audience:

GOLDBERG: . . . You're a capable man, McCann.
MCCANN: That's a great compliment, Nat, coming from a man in your position.
GOLDBERG: Well, I've got a position, I won't deny it.
MCCANN: You certainly have.
GOLDBERG: I would never deny that I had a position.
MCCANN: And what a position!
GOLDBERG: It's not a thing I would deny. (pp. 44–5)

The comic contrast of Jew and Irishman is pushed to the limit:

MCCANN: You've always been a true Christian.
GOLDBERG: In a way. (p. 45)

Generally McCann is a quiet, brooding and menacing presence, while Goldberg dominates the stage with a series of marvellously evocative reminiscences of a glorious childhood filled with happy sunny days and great family affection. These speeches (on pp. 41, 43, 73, 76–7, 102 and 108) are worth careful consideration because they are so important in defining Goldberg's character and function. They are made up entirely of clichés, using the phrasing and rhythm of the cockney Jew. Any section might be quoted to suggest the tone, as here:

Uncle Barney. Of course, he was an impeccable dresser. One of the old school. He had a house just outside Basingstoke at the time. Respected by the whole community. Culture? Don't talk to me about culture.

He was an all-round man, what do you mean? He was a cosmopolitan. (p. 42)

On one level the sheer exuberance of all this, and its closeness to parody, makes Goldberg something of a wonderful joke. But Goldberg isn't a joke. He is on a nasty mission, and these very speeches are constantly being undermined from within by a demolishing bathos:

Humming away I'd be, past the children's playground. I'd tip my hat to the toddlers, I'd give a helping hand to a couple of stray dogs, everything came natural. I can see it like yesterday. The sun falling behind the dog stadium. Ah! (p. 73)

The performance aspect of these speeches is also highlighted by the swift change to officious gobbledegook when McCann is desperate for reassurance: 'GOLDBERG: The main issue is a singular issue and quite distinct from your previous work. Certain elements, however, might well approximate . . .' (p. 46). Goldberg's ability to switch easily from one register to another, depending on who he is addressing, points to the danger of the character.

Guido Almansi, writing about 'Harold Pinter's Idiom of Lies', doesn't find Goldberg funny at all. For him, the clichés are both repulsive and disgusting, the product of a deranged mind. Goldberg's 'complacent self-satisfied articulation of rotting fragments from a language of null feeling and null sensibility succeeds in creating a full-fledged character, obscene because he uses language at its most common denominator' (*Stratford-upon-Avon Studies*, 19, Contemporary English Drama, 1981, p. 88). Katherine Worth justifies Goldberg's language more in keeping with how and why he collapses in Act Three. She recognises how Jewish elements are carefully selected in Goldberg's speeches to build up cumulatively 'a strange mask of Jewishness' and, she concludes, 'In coming to these deliberate effects of staginess we come to the heart of Pinter's drama, it seems to me. He uses false voices, phoney performances as a writer like O'Neill uses masks. And for a similar purpose, to convey the terrible sense of non-identity and disconnectedness that almost all his characters, like O'Neill's, suffer from' (*Casebook*, p. 37).

Goldberg's hysterical reaction to McCann's paper-tearing in Act Three, his being called 'Simey', and his first realisation of physical decline ('I don't know why, but I feel knocked out. I feel a bit . . . It's uncommon for me.' p. 145) all indicate that the structure of belief and past certainties, which has sustained him, is empty. The cliché-ridden values – 'Play up, play up, and play the game. Honour thy father and thy mother. All along the line' – lose their conviction and he is left as bereft as anybody:

> Because I believe that the world . . . (*Vacant*) . . .
> Because I believe that the world . . . (*Desperate*) . . .
> BECAUSE I BELIEVE THAT THE WORLD . . . (*Lost*) . . .
> (p. 144)

STANLEY AND THE VISITORS In Act Two Stanley confronts McCann and Goldberg in two separate dualogues before being subject to their combined verbal assault. The dualogues show Stanley to be a cornered victim and the dramatic force of these encounters derives from various theatrical devices. Most effectively, the element of the unknown is present. Why have Goldberg and McCann appeared, and what has Stanley done? It is not entirely appropriate to call the unknown a 'subtext' here, because it is all too *obvious* that both Stanley and McCann, to begin with, know far more than they admit.

The tactic employed by McCann is to behave as if nothing is untoward. A mood is created initially by the stage picture – '*McCann is sitting at the table tearing a sheet of newspaper into five equal strips*' (p. 61). This, inevitably, takes some time and develops suspense. As Irving Wardle explains, 'This device is an extreme example of the playwright's habit of introducing an intrinsically theatrical idea and letting it find its own road back towards common sense. Mr Pinter's way is the opposite of setting out deliberately to embody a theme in action' (*Casebook*, p. 111). Thereafter, during the scene, the strips of paper are a latent threat to Stanley.

> STANLEY *walks round the table towards the door.*
> McCANN *meets him.*
> STANLEY: Excuse me.
> McCANN: Where are you going?
> STANLEY: I want to go out.
> McCANN: Why don't you stay here?
> STANLEY *moves away, to the right of the table.*
> STANLEY: So you're down here on holiday?
> McCANN: A short one. (STANLEY *picks up a strip of paper.* McCANN *moves in.*)
> Mind that.
> STANLEY: What is it?
> McCANN: Mind it. Leave it. (p. 65)

In a kind of perverted game, McCann's words are full of solicitude and polite concern, but they take on precisely the opposite effect as the two men circle the table and Stanley is warned to keep away from the strips of paper. McCann's very presence, a stranger in the room, is an implicit threat, and his confidence causes Stanley progressively to plead his 'innocence'. McCann doesn't accuse him of anything, but keeps control by physical intervention – animal-like – and deadpan replies:

> STANLEY: I'm sorry. I'm not in the mood for a party tonight.
> MCCANN: Oh, is that so? I'm sorry.
> STANLEY: Yes, I'm going out to celebrate quietly, on my own.
> MCCANN: That's a shame.
> *They stand.* (p. 63)

Stanley's fear is compounded by the '*Voices from the back*', which he knows involve Goldberg, and Stanley is sure that Goldberg knows more than McCann – 'Has he told you anything? Do you know what you're here for?' (p. 71).

The scene is riveting because of the effect of McCann's controlled violence and his refusal to accuse Stanley of anything. It forces Stanley to expressions of self-justification which sound increasingly suspect (see pp. 67–8). The paranoia that he has suffered since first hearing of the visitation now carries the conviction of guilt, albeit unspecified – 'I mean you wouldn't think, to look at me, really . . . I mean, not really, that I was the sort of bloke to – to cause any trouble, would you?' (p. 68). And he is reduced to the most banal attempt at appeasing McCann – 'I know Ireland very well. I've many friends there. I love that country and I admire and trust its people' (p. 72). The clichés of this speech underline how much of the language used by both characters is strategic. The attack and defence mechanisms are partly physical (with McCann protecting his strips of paper) but mostly linguistic: Stanley

lying and pleading, and McCann non-committal or
diverting any direct question:

> STANLEY: I've got a feeling we've met before.
> McCANN: No we haven't.
> STANLEY: Ever been anywhere near Maidenhead?
> McCANN: No.
> STANLEY: There's a Fuller's tea shop. I used to have
> my tea there.
> McCANN: I don't know it. (pp. 65–6)

Having got nowhere with McCann, Stanley becomes
more aggressive when he is left alone with Goldberg
(p. 75). Again, to begin with Goldberg withholds direct
assault and accusation and merely parries Stanley's
demands:

> STANLEY: . . . You'll have to find somewhere else.
> GOLDBERG: Are you the manager here?
> STANLEY: That's right.
> GOLDBERG: Is it a good game? (p. 76)

The scene moves, as does the play, remorselessly, towards
a positive assault on Stanley, and this would be less
effective if Stanley was a completely defenceless victim.
However, he knows he is threatened and does make an
effort to survive ('Let me – just make this clear. You don't
bother me. To me, you're nothing but a dirty joke . . .'
pp. 77–8). He has failed to divert McCann and Goldberg
in their two dualogues but he resists as long as he can
in the cat-and-mouse challenge of 'sitting down' which
precedes his interrogation:

> GOLDBERG: McCann.
> McCANN: Nat?

GOLDBERG: Ask him to sit down.

MCCANN: Yes, Nat. (MCCANN *moves to* STANLEY.) Do you mind sitting down?

STANLEY: Yes, I do mind. (p. 79)

The implied threat of physical violence, with two against one, makes a disturbing stage picture – and the more disturbing because of the lack of actual violence. Stanley has no option but to sit down, and the interrogation begins. This moves the play into a shockingly different level of 'realism'.

The play begins with a perfectly conventional setting – the living room – and recognisable characters. The visitors add a dimension of the surreal by combining a stylised language, a stage double-act, and an unspecified mission which is obviously related to a pursuit of Stanley. Now they throw all their combined venom at him in a joint verbal assault which accuses him of being 'wrong'. The effect of the relentless barrage is nightmarish. The catalogue of crimes begins with references that an audience will immediately pick up from earlier in the play – his lethargy and his treatment of Meg, Petey and Lulu. Thereafter the questions and accusations become increasingly bizarre and improbable. McCann, the Irish-man, focuses on the betrayal of 'the organisation', of Ireland and the Church; Goldberg concentrates on Stanley's family failings and his uncleanness; but they also throw in questions that are unanswerable:

MCCANN: What about the Albigensenist heresy?

GOLDBERG: Who watered the wicket in Melbourne?

MCCANN: What about the blessed Oliver Plunkett?

GOLDBERG: Speak up, Webber. Why did the chicken cross the road? (p. 92)

The force of the inquisition derives partly from the staccato form and the variety of non-stop detailed accusations, but also from the sheer aural assault where the rhythm produces a mental torture that breaks Stanley down. A similarly non-naturalistic sequence occurs in Act Three when the two accusers reverse the procedure and *'begin to woo him, gently and with relish'* (p. 152):

> GOLDBERG: From now on, we'll be the hub of your wheel.
> MCCANN: We'll renew your season ticket.
> GOLDBERG: We'll take tuppence off your morning tea.
> MCCANN: We'll give you a discount on all inflammable goods.
> GOLDBERG: We'll watch over you.
> MCCANN: Advise you.
> GOLDBERG: Give you proper care and treatment.
> (pp. 153–4)

During the first sequence of accusations Stanley tries to respond but is shouted down until he screams; during the second sequence Stanley remains completely silent. In both passages the play is taken onto a level of symbolism by the shift in the structure of the language, but the action reverts to naturalism with the respective entrances of Meg (p. 95) and Petey (p. 159).

The Birthday Party: In Conclusion

The Birthday Party, Pinter's first full-length play, is often linked with *The Room* and *The Dumb Waiter* because of its movement from comedy to menace. The comedy emerges from the silliness of Meg and the bonhomie of Goldberg. Menace is introduced by Goldberg and

McCann who pose a threat to Stanley and eventually break him down. The originality of the play derives from its language and from the fact that the action operates on more than one level. Both the language and the action are in stark contrast to the surface naturalism and ordinariness of the conventional stage setting – in this case a seaside boarding house.

Pinter's dialogue shows how much of speech is strategic, purposeful and far removed from everyday chit-chat. Rarely do Pinter's characters engage in straightforward conversation. Characters are mostly using language for purposes of self-defence or domination, which points to their essential insecurity and isolation. The birthday party, at the centre of the play, is wholly ironic (and disturbing) because what should be a happy social celebration becomes a macabre travesty, with Stanley a silent victim and all the other characters preoccupied with private obsessions.

On one level the play operates as a thriller, with Stanley cast as the guilty man and Goldberg and McCann as the agents of justice. However, the play takes a more powerful imaginative hold on the audience because it bypasses rational explanations (concerning the background and motivation and characters) and makes Stanley the pathetic victim of a ruthless assault by the agents of the social and religious 'establishment' which demands conformity to their rules. Stanley has opted out of conventional responsibilities and after a brief defiance is unable to withstand the physical threat and verbal assault to which he is subjected. A further disturbing element in the action is that Goldberg and McCann, the ominous and powerful combined force, are also shown to be deeply insecure individuals. Finally, the play offers an intense and frightening metaphor for the underlying fear that the sensitive individual has of the 'outside world', with its various demands.

Textual Notes

Act One

1 *The living-room . . .* – There is no mention in this stage direction of the house being a 'boarding house', which Meg claims. Stanley denies that in any business sense it is: he is the only lodger. This confusion adds to the possibility that the action could happen anywhere. All the place names suggest that the house is in a seaside town on the south coast of England, within reasonably easy reach of London.

During the play, the movement of the characters in the room is meticulously choreographed. The use of doors for entrances and exits, the hatch, the table and chairs is always mentioned in the text. It is advisable to have a picture of the stage in mind when reading the play, especially when it comes to characters sitting and standing which may indicate positions of relative strength and domination between them on stage.

Stage directions (in italics in these notes) relate to the conventional theatre practice of assuming that you are standing on the stage, facing the audience; so 'stage left' is in fact on the right from the view of the audience. Also 'upstage' and 'downstage' refer to the back and front of the stage respectively.

3 the old chairs – Petey is employed as a deckchair attendant at the seaside.

4 *beginning to darn* – a detail which 'dates' the play. Darning (repairing holes in woollen socks) is rarely done these days.

5 Lady Mary Splatt – a double joke is intended here: 'Splatt' is a most unsophisticated name for a 'Lady', and Meg's reply, 'I don't know her', is ingenuous.

7 Fried bread – this, on its own, would be a very meagre breakfast.

9 This house is on the list – the list of approved lodgings prepared for the benefit of tourists.

– You've got a room ready? – Petey's question hints that he is unsure, as if the house is not used to visitors. Stanley claims he is the only one to have stayed there.

10 the Palace – a popular name for a theatre.

– the pier – a feature of many seaside towns: a construction stretching into the sea which carries amusements for holidaymakers.

– a straight show – a play, as opposed to a variety entertainment.

12 STANLEY *enters* – Stanley's entrance is likely to be surprising. Meg has twice referred to that 'boy', which Stanley is not. His appearance indicates his slovenliness. His glasses are a significant detail because they become a motif in the play: Stanley is going to be made to 'see straight'.

13 milk's off – the milk is sour.

15 on the front – adjacent to the sea (i.e. the fashionable part of town): a most improbable threat from Stanley.

18 succulent – a typical example of Pinteresque word-play, where a completely innocuous word meaning juicy is given sexual overtones by Meg's reaction.

20 the strap – a leather strap used for punishing
children, now illegal.

23 I've had some lovely afternoons in that room –
Meg's claim has given rise to the possibility of a
sexual relationship between her and Stanley:
however, his treatment of her in this scene suggests
otherwise. Nevertheless, her physical and emotional
attachment could be having a psychological effect
on Stanley.

24 *A pause.* STANLEY *slowly raises his head.* – All
stage directions in a Pinter play are as significant as
any spoken word: here the impact of Meg's
mentioning 'two gentlemen' is registered.

26 taking the Michael – more often expressed as
'taking the micky' (making fun of).
a false alarm – this emphasises the extent of
Stanley's concern. Why should visitors seeking a
seaside boarding house be 'alarming'?

28 Tell me, Mrs Boles . . . – Stanley introduces the
issue of his 'identity'.

30 all found – all subsistence (food and
accommodation) included.

31 Lower Edmonton – a suburban area of North
London, not associated with any significant concert
hall.
 – the lot – an all-embracing term suggesting
extravagant celebration.

32 A fast one – a deliberate trick; Stanley suggests that
he was deceived.
 – All right, Jack – a colloquial reference to nobody in
particular.
 – I can take a tip – take a hint.
 – rock cake – a dismissive term in this context.

32 pay a visit – go to the lavatory. Meg interprets Stanley's physical gestures of discomfort as indigestion, whereas they are more indicative of a much deeper psychological distress, brought on by the news of the impending visitors and his sense that they must be coming for him.

33 van/wheelbarrow – Stanley's frightening of Meg (and projecting his own fear) is an example of why the play is regarded as a 'comedy of menace'. On a more serious level the van and wheelbarrow have been interpreted as representing a hearse and a coffin, and the visitors ('they') as representing death – thus presaging the arrival of Goldberg and McCann.

34 *A sudden knock* – provides a vivid climax to the foregoing dialogue.

35 *whispers* – the whispering and the 'parcel' both add to the development of suspense that is being generated on stage.

37 compact – a small make-up container.

38 under her feet – Lulu's accusation tells the audience that Stanley rarely leaves the house.

40 a washout – a hopeless failure: this is one of the first accusations levelled at Stanley by Goldberg (see p. 84).

 – *Enter Goldberg and McCann* – these characters should be immediately identifiable as a (cockney) Jew and an Irishman by their different accents.

41 Brighton, Canvey Island, Rottingdean – all popular resorts for London day-trippers in the 1950s.

 – Shabbuss – Saturday, the Jewish Sabbath.

42 One of the old school – someone who upholds old-fashioned or traditional habits of appearance and behaviour.

- Basingstoke – a town in Hampshire, south-west of
London. Seemingly insignificant at this moment, it
is likely to register strongly when Stanley says that
he used to live there (p. 72): this is one of several
clues that Stanley and Goldberg have a connection
in the past.

42 the right house – McCann's question makes
Goldberg the more sinister when he replies 'I wasn't
looking for a number' – what was he looking for?

43 coppers – a small amount of money (literally: coins
of small denomination.

- MCC – Marylebone Cricket Club. A touring
English cricket team used the title MCC when not
playing test matches in the 1950s.

- my name was good – Goldberg says that his name
alone was a sufficient guarantee in business
dealings.

- do a job – the unspecified nature of 'the job' makes
it all the more sinister.

- cool as a whistle – calm and controlled.

44 they approached me – Goldberg and McCann's
employers remain a mystery.

45 a true Christian – the menace of the two intruders is
tinged with comedy: Goldberg is very obviously
Jewish.

46 The main issue . . . Satisfied? – the shift in register
(style of speech) is disturbing. Goldberg speaks
officious gobbledegook which is unspecific in detail
but which does confirm that the two are on a
'mission'.

47 let rooms – hire rooms.

50 Does he play a nice piano? – Does he play the piano
well?

- MEG: (*falteringly*) In . . . a big hall . . . came down here.' – see p. 45–6 of this book for comment on this speech.
52 If we hadn't come today we'd have come tomorrow – the suggestion of inevitability sounds ominous.
53 McCann's the life and soul of any party – there should be no mistaking the comic effect of this unlikely claim.
- We'll bring him out of himself – a very ironic comment given what Goldberg and McCann do to Stanley in the play.
60 *his face and the drumbeat now savage and possessed* – this climax to Act One shows the extent to which Stanley has been disturbed psychologically by the arrival of Goldberg and McCann.

Act Two
61 *McCann is sitting . . .* – see p. 68 of this book for further comment.
63 '*The Mountains of Morne*' – an Irish folk song.
65 Maidenhead – a town west of London.
- Fuller's teashop, Boots library – these references are repeated by Goldberg on p. 102, which hints at a past connection between him and Stanley (though any such connection is never actually substantiated).
68 the man of the house – an expression for the householder, in this case Petey.
70 Round the bend – mad.
71 What you're at – what you mean.
72 Basingstoke – the proliferation of names of places associated with Stanley's past add confusion to his identity. However, none of the towns are especially

remarkable, which enhances the 'ordinariness' of Stanley.

72 draught Guinness – the beer most famously associated with Ireland.

73 I was telling Mr Boles . . . – for comment on Goldberg's language, see this book, pp. 65–7.

74 a peck – a small kiss.

– Carrikmacross – an Irish town north-west of Dublin.

– Simey – Goldberg is also called Nat and Benny in the play, which adds confusion to his identity.

– gefilte fish – a fish dish traditionally popular in Jewish homes.

76 booked out – all the rooms have been reserved.

– a good game – a successful business.

77 crabby – dirty.

– boghouse – a vulgar term for lavatory.

– unlicensed premises – an establishment in Britain requires a licence to sell alcohol. As this is not McCann's intention Stanley's words indicate his desperation.

78 get on my breasts – a version of the colloquial 'get on my tits', meaning 'to annoy me'.

– Sit down – this begins a Pinteresque power struggle in the form of a stylised game: there is still a comic dimension to the undoubted menace.

81 I'll kick the shite out of him! – (shite = shit, excrement) McCann is more physically aggressive than Goldberg who remains in control and is not looking for an actual fight.

82 Webber, what were you doing yesterday? – the interrogation of Stanley (pp. 82–94) includes many obscure references that are juxtaposed irrationally:

the dramatic force of the assault derives partly from
the build-up of the bizarre accusations but more
from the insistent rhythm of the two voices brow-
beating the hapless Stanley.

82 washout – Goldberg uses the same term as Lulu
(p. 40).

– on everybody's wick – nerves.

– off her conk – mad, insane.

83 'the organisation' . . . 'betray us' . . . 'Black and Tan
fact' – McCann's accusations derive from his Irish
background: they are not specific, any more than
Goldberg's are, but they are cumulative in effect and
appropriate to the character. A fanatical republican
would regard the 'betrayal' of a nationalist
organisation (such as the IRA) as a great crime.
'Black and Tans' were the British soldiers sent to
repress Irish nationalist uprisings in 1919–20, which
they did with great force, earning a lasting hatred.

– the wrong horse – mistaken.

84 Enos or Andrews – brand names of liver salts
usually taken to ease indigestion.

85 Take off his glasses – Stanley's glasses have been
part of his identity from his first entrance, and
remain so throughout the play. For Goldberg and
McCann to attack Stanley by way of his eyes is
particularly unpleasant.

86 Lyon's Corner House – a popular chain of London
restaurants no longer in existence.

– Marble Arch – a place in central London, where
Oxford Street meets Park Lane.

88 the porch – church entrance.

– skedaddled – ran away.

– in the lurch – in trouble.

- the pudding club – pregnant.

90 We're right and you're wrong, Webber, all along the line. – regardless of the many accusations thrown at Stanley, this line encapsulates the essence of the interrogation. Stanley is a 'guilty' man. This is discussed in the commentary on the play.

91 a building society – a savings bank that lends money for house purchases.

- traitor to the cloth – a priest who is unfaithful to his vows.

92 Albigensenist heresy – refers to a twelfth-century challenge to Christian orthodoxy by a group of reformers living in Albi in Languedoc, France.

- watered the wicket in Melbourne – refers to a cricket test-match wicket being illegally watered to provide an unfair advantage to the bowling side.

- blessed Oliver Plunkett – an Irish martyr.

93 Drogheda – the site of a particularly brutal assault on Irish loyalist supporters by Oliver Cromwell in 1649.

94 Judas – the disciple who betrayed Jesus.

95 *loud drumbeat off left* – a very theatrical climax which heralds a new 'movement' to the play's action – the birthday party.

96 Could I have my glasses? – the last articulate line spoken by Stanley.

- *He holds them out* – this exchange of glasses indicates the control that Goldberg has managed to achieve over Stanley.

- Enough to scuttle a liner – enough drink to sink a ship.

- Scotch, Irish – different types of whiskies: the Irish is for McCann.

97 Walk up the boulevard . . . – the comedy of this
   stage business is in marked contrast to the condition
   of the silent Stanley.

 – Gladiola – a brightly coloured flower.

99 *Outside the window there is still a faint light* – the
   atmosphere of menace throughout the remainder of
   the act is greatly enhanced by the lighting changes,
   both exterior and interior.

102 A little Austin – a popular make of car in the 1950s.
    tea in Fuller's, book from Boots – Goldberg echoes
    Stanley, see p. 66.

 – on our tod – alone.

 – to kip on – sleep on.

 – Mazoltov – Yiddish expression for 'good luck'.

 – Simchas – Yiddish for happy occasions.

103 well over the fast – keep well (over the days of
    fasting).

104 They were all there that night – these are the same
    words used by Stanley when describing his concert,
    see p. 31.

105 mixing them – i.e. mixing Scotch and Irish whiskies.

107 King's Cross – noted for its famous railway station:
    Meg is not on the same wavelength as McCann and
    their separate reveries, under the influence of drink,
    heighten the isolation of Stanley, who is ignored.

108 Gesundheit – cheers.

 – constitutional – a healthy walk.

110 Roscrea, Mother Nolan's . . . night-light . . . My
    little room – Meg, McCann, Goldberg and Lulu
    revert to their past during the party, where they
    form an almost chorus-like group of vastly 'separate'
    identities, nobody understanding anybody else.

111 Tullamore – an Irish town.

- bold Fenian men – 'Fenian' was the name given to Irish freedom fighters.
113 Blind man's buff – a children's game in which a blindfolded player has to touch another who is then blindfolded in turn. What should be fun takes on a very macabre dimension.

Act Three
122 *The next morning . . .* – an echo of the opening scene of the play but more disturbing at first because there is no reference to the night's events.
132 a few letters after his name – letters that indicate professional or academic qualifications.
   - Dermot – McCann is also Seamus in the play.
134 Abdullah – a Turkish cigarette.
138 Monty – if Monty is the employer, the authority-figure responsible for Goldberg and McCann, he remains a mystery.
139 my peas – it has been noted that Petey's decision to tend his garden is the first occasion that Goldberg becomes really agitated.
142 the thing done – we are not told what this 'thing' is. What has happened to Stanley overnight and what is going to happen to him is left to our imagination.
144 Play up, play up, and play the game – from the poem 'Vitaï Lampada' by Henry Newbolt which advocates the public school spirit and compares warfare to cricket.
   - Honour thy father and thy mother – one of the ten commandments (Exodus 20: 12).
144 Follow my mental? – Do you understand me?
   - don't go too near the water – be careful.
145 low lives, schnorrers, layabouts – worthless people.

    – the good book – the Bible.

146 One for the road – an expression usually applied to a last drink before going home.

    – got the needle – angry.

    – pontoon – a card game.

148 schmulu – an endearment. Rhyming with Lulu it is Yiddish wordplay.

149 a jump ahead – more sexually experienced.

150 Confess! – confession of sins is a sacrament of the Catholic Church.

    – unfrocked – removed from the priesthood, usually for some wrongdoing.

    – Rock of Cashel – a holy site in Tipperary, Ireland.

    – *Ushers in Stanley* – Stanley's appearance accords with social orthodox respectability (in marked contrast to his first entrance). In the Royal National Theatre's 1994 production Goldberg, McCann and Stanley were all dressed the same and looked like undertakers.

152 Somewhere over the rainbow – a Utopian ideal (Judy Garland made the song famous in the film *The Wizard of Oz*).

    – Where angels fear to tread – from Alexander Pope's *An Essay on Criticism* (1711): 'For fools rush in where angels fear to tread.' It is also the title of a novel by E. M. Forster. This specific reference, as above and throughout the extended litany of comfort by Goldberg and McCann, is less important than the cumulative effect, which is a reversal of the breaking-down of Stanley in Act Two.

154 tuppence – refers to two old pennies.

    – club bar – the bar that is exclusive to members of a club.

- a table reserved – as in an exclusive restaurant.
155 hot tips – gambling advice.
156 on the house – free of charge.
157 mensch – one of the people (German).
158 *Sounds from his throat* – Pinter has said that these sounds indicate that Stanley 'is trying to go further. He is on the edge of utterance. But it's a long, impossible edge . . .' (*V.V.*, p. 10)
161 Stan, don't let them tell you what to do! – In 1988 Pinter said that this 'is one of the most important lines I've ever written. I've lived with that line all my damn life. Never more than now.' (*Gussow*, p. 71)
163 belle of the ball – see this book, p. 45.

The Caretaker

Synopsis

The Caretaker takes place in an upstairs room of a derelict house in West London. The room is crammed with miscellaneous objects (the collection of Aston, who lives in the room). These include an iron bed, paint buckets, boxes containing nuts, screws, etc., a stepladder, coal bucket, lawnmower and gas stove, on which is placed a statue of Buddha. The full list is given on p. vii of the text. This is all defined by Aston's brother, Mick, as 'junk'.

ACT ONE (a night in winter) Mick, a man in his late twenties, is sitting on a bed silently looking at the objects around him. When he hears a door bang downstairs, and muffled voices, he makes a hasty exit. He is not to be seen again until the very end of the act. Two men enter the room: Aston, a man in his early thirties (who is Mick's brother), and Davies, an old tramp. We learn that Aston has rescued Davies from a fight in the café where he had been working as an odd-job man. Davies has been sacked for making 'a commotion'. Aston is in charge of the house but lives in this one room. He makes Davies welcome, offers him tobacco, a pair of shoes, a bed for the night and even some money. Aston is planning to clear the garden and build a shed. Davies says that he is waiting for the weather to improve so that he can get to Sidcup and reclaim his 'papers', which he needs to confirm who he is. In contrast to Aston, who is quiet and introspective, Davies is extremely voluble, questioning and opinionated. In the morning Aston tells Davies that he was making noises in his sleep, which Davies strenuously denies. When Aston prepares to go out to purchase a saw Davies rushes to leave with him, but is invited to stay and given a key. Davies says he will try to get a job in a café in Wembley later in the day. When Aston leaves and Davies begins to examine the objects in the room, Mick re-appears, silently, and attacks the tramp, throwing him to the floor. He demands to know 'What's the game?'

ACT TWO Davies is still on the floor with Mick watching him. Mick baffles and frightens Davies with a series of searching questions and elaborate monologues, in which he claims that Davies reminds him of various people in his past. He says the house is his and offers to let it to Davies for a reasonable rent. Aston returns with a bag he has bought to replace the one Davies had left at the café. Mick grabs it, but when Aston shows that he wants Davies to have it Mick leaves the room. Aston says that he is supposed to be decorating the landing and making a flat out of it for his brother, who is in the building trade. He offers Davies a job as caretaker. Davies is hesitant – wary in case this involves actual work.

Later, Davies enters the room in darkness (the light switch not working). Suddenly a vacuum cleaner starts to hum and in the dark it is used by Mick to terrify Davies. Mick then adopts a friendly manner, offers Davies a sandwich, and confides that he is worried about his brother's inactivity. He also offers Davies a job as care-taker. Davies is confused about who owns the room, but is deceived by Mick, who asks him for references. Davies says he can get them from Sidcup.

In the morning Aston wakes Davies so that he can go to Sidcup. Davies starts complaining about the draught from the window and the bad weather, which he makes an excuse for not going out. Aston then delivers a long, hesitant speech in which he tells of his experience of being forced to undergo electric shock treatment in a mental hospital. He is surprised that he didn't die. Following his treatment he has avoided talking to people and is intent on building his shed in the garden.

ACT THREE (two weeks later) Davies complains to Mick that Aston has been ignoring him and has denied him a bread knife and a clock. Mick takes little notice and imagines what a penthouse he could make of 'this place' for himself and his brother. Davies wants Mick to intercede between him and Aston, and suggests that he is the person to help with the decorating. However, when the door bangs downstairs announcing the return of Aston, Mick immediately leaves. Davies begrudgingly accepts a pair of shoes that Aston has brought for him.

At night Davies is groaning in his sleep. He is woken by Aston who can't sleep for the noise. Davies reacts furiously and turns viciously against Aston, threatening him with a return to the hospital, which he calls a 'nuthouse'. Aston responds quietly, saying that he wants Davies to leave because 'I don't think we're hitting it off.' Davies leaves, believing that Mick will help him. When Davies returns with Mick he argues for the eviction of Aston. Mick says that this would be a possibility if Davies proves to be as good an interior decorator as he claims. When Davies admits that he isn't, Mick pretends surprise and disappointment. He smashes the figure of Buddha, and dismisses Davies with a half-crown for his 'care-taking'. Aston returns and faces Mick, '*Both are smiling, faintly*'. Mick leaves, and Davies tries desperately to win back Aston's favour. Aston doesn't respond, saying simply, 'You make too much noise.'

The Play

To say that *The Caretaker* is a play about two brothers and a tramp is a reasonable starting point. The interaction between these three is what holds our attention when watching or reading the play. The intensity of the action and emotions and the richness of language do, however, open the play to speculative interpretations about life in general, and life in 1950s England in particular. Pinter has always insisted that 'I don't think of themes when I'm writing', but he is equally aware that 'theatre has always been a critical act, looking in a broad sense at the society in which we live and attempting to reflect and dramatise these findings' (*Gussow*, p. 123). It is unlikely that a seventeenth-century audience would have left a perfor-mance of *King Lear* discussing the theme of 'Nature' that was explored in the play, but that is not to deny that such a theme exists. Pinter writes instinctively and, as he says, follows the clues that his characters present to him. So, for example, he did have the notion that the play would end violently, possibly with a death, but he discovered that when the end came this is not what happens. The first priority in writing a play is one of giving life to the characters, but this does not preclude a wider appreciation of human behaviour and the life of the time, which critics and teachers find convenient to discuss under the heading of 'themes'. In the theatre the play is about two brothers and a tramp; on reflection, the play communicates on a variety of levels. The content of the play and its themes emerge from a consideration of what 'kind' of play *The Caretaker* is, but this is not easy to define.

Speaking in 1961, Pinter was aware of the British theatre moving away from traditional forms: 'it seems to me that there has been a certain development in one channel or another in the past three years. *The Caretaker* wouldn't have been put on, and certainly wouldn't have run, before 1957. The old categories of comedy and tragedy and farce are irrelevant, and the fact that managers seem to have realised that is one favourable change' (*Plays Two*, p. xi). The realistic details of *The Caretaker*, visual and linguistic, clearly place the play in the tradition of naturalism – as was examined in Chapter One of this book. However, there are comic elements and serious elements which move the play at times towards comedy and at times towards tragedy. Plays that combine these elements have become a feature in European drama during the twentieth century, following Anton Chekhov, and tragicomedy is recognised in the work of Sean O'Casey, J. M. Synge and some of Pirandello; Beckett's *Waiting for Godot* is defined as 'a tragicomedy in two acts'. However Beckett's play is also synonymous with the 'Theatre of the Absurd', and the existentialist elements of characters living in a godless universe have also been recognised in the *The Caretaker*. Pinter's play includes elements of all these forms.

Realistic elements
From the beginning of *The Caretaker*, realistic detail is a most striking feature. The setting of an attic room filled

with a vast amount of clutter, all easily identifiable, has to be taken as a place where somebody lives. It is far removed from the elegant country-house setting which the critic Kenneth Tynan lamented was usual on the 1950s West-End stage. The physical details of the room are used in the most natural way up until Mick hurls the Buddha statue against the gas stove. Aston busies himself trying to mend a plug and a toaster; a bed is prepared for Davies; there is considerable discussion relating to the one window and whether it should be open or not; a bucket hangs from the ceiling and collects actual drips; Mick uses the electrolux to frighten Davies; Davies' clothing – his trousers, his jacket and shoes and the all-purpose bag for his belongings – are all employed dramatically. In fact much of the play shows characters *using* the objects and clothing for dramatic purposes. Invariably a significant point of character development is expressed by the way a very ordinary object is used. For example, the handing over of a door key shows the extent of Aston's goodwill, and Mick deceives Davies into a false sense of security by the device of a cheese sandwich. Ultimately, the cumulative effect of focusing on the details of the room is to heighten the importance of the room itself, which becomes the object of Davies' ambition and his downfall.

The room is not an oasis. There is a suggestion that society does not intrude in a Pinter play, only people do. However, in *The Caretaker*, there is a continuous motif of place-names and local landmarks which keep the characters in a very real world. This is 1950s urban London, which is always being evoked in a legion of references: the North Circular, the Great West Road, Sidcup, Acton and so on. This environment reaches a level close to celebration in Mick's marvellous prose-poem (pp. 46–7):

MICK: You know, believe it or not, you've got a funny
kind of resemblance to a bloke I once knew in
Shoreditch. Actually he lived in Aldgate. I was
staying with a cousin in Camden Town. This chap,
he used to have a pitch in Finsbury Park, just by the
bus depot. When I got to know him I found out he
was brought up in Putney . . .

Both Aston and Davies fill in details of their life outside
the room in terms of places visited. Aston refers to visiting
a pub and 'a kind of shop' which sells second-hand tools,
and avoiding a particular café; and Davies' life is entirely
made up of visits from one place to another – a monastery
in Luton, a convenience in Shepherd's Bush, a caff in
Wembley. The universal significance of their experience is
made the more telling by the actuality of where they live.

This environment of a specific room in a defined
locality provides a realistic setting for an exploration of
characters who are each granted an intense psychological
realism, mainly through the medium of language.
Traditionally when playwrights in the English theatre
have staged 'the poor', or characters from 'the working
class', it has been either patronisingly or with a political
agenda. That neither of these directions interests Pinter is
shown immediately with the entrance of Aston and
Davies. There is no 'exposition', setting up themes or
contrived dramatic conflicts, simply an invitation:

ASTON: Sit down.
DAVIES: Thanks. (*Looking about*) Uuh . . .
ASTON: Just a minute.
    ASTON *looks around for a chair, sees one lying on its
    side by the rolled carpet at the fireplace, and starts to
    get it out.*

DAVIES: Sit down? Huh . . . I haven't had a good sit
down . . . I haven't had a proper sit down . . . well, I
couldn't tell you . . .
ASTON: (*placing the chair*) Here you are. (p. 2)

The characters are introduced in a totally realistic manner,
with the stage business of finding a chair complementing
the realism of Davies' unfinished sentences. Thereafter,
throughout the play, Davies' language has a vivid
authenticity which grips our attention and keeps the
dramatic focus entirely on the three people on stage. The
meticulous degree of realism attached to the characters
and their language is covered in the sections below.

Comic elements

The Caretaker, like a number of Pinter plays, begins with
a lot of humour but moves into a more sombre key.
Comedy surrounds Davies the tramp – in his appearance
and his language – but there is also a comic dimension to
the linguistic strategies of Mick. Virtually no comedy,
however, relates to the introverted Aston.

Davies has become renowned as one of the great
modern stage characters and one of the most original. This
has occasionally distorted audience reaction to the play
because some of the stage business and the comic lines are
so well known that they are anticipated, and audiences
have been known to look for the comedy more than
anything else. Essentially, of course, Davies isn't trying to
be funny at any time. In this respect he differs from
another great comic character of the low-life, Shakespeare's Falstaff. In *Henry IV* Falstaff is a massive life-
force, a bundle of sin and anti-social behaviour, but he is
also a wit and tinged with genius. As such he is a source of

great pleasure (as he says, 'I am not only witty in myself, but the cause that wit is in other men'). Falstaff knows well how to put on a good show for the entertainment of his fellows in the Eastcheap tavern in order to avoid censure and having to pay the bill. He knows when he is being funny. The comedy emanating from Davies in *The Caretaker* is, however, never intentional.

At one extreme there is a farcical element to the comedy, as when Davies is caught literally with no trousers on at the end of the first act, and chased around the room in this condition at the start of the second act. Other physical and visual comedy occurs when Davies tries on the shoes and the smoking-jacket. On p. 15 of the text Davies is offered a pair of shoes by Aston and as he tries them on his praise for their quality is eloquent – so eloquent in fact that it leads quite unconsciously to a very good joke, especially if the actor gets the timing right:

> DAVIES: Not a bad pair of shoes. (*He trudges round the room.*) They're strong, all right. Yes. Not a bad shape of shoe. This leather's hardy, en't? Very hardy. Some bloke tried to flog me some suede the other day. I wouldn't wear them. Can't beat leather, for wear. Suede goes off, it creases, it stains for life in five minutes. You can't beat leather. Yes. Good shoe this.
> ASTON: Good.
> DAVIES *wiggles his feet.*
> DAVIES: Don't fit though.

The performance involved in trying on a 'smoking-jacket' (p. 65) – a wholly inappropriate garment for a tramp – is also ripe for comedy. The visual comedy relates to Davies as a stage personality, and to an extent on our enjoyment of an actor's performance. Indeed we are always at a safe distance from the unsavoury aspects of Davies precisely because he is a character on stage and not living in our kitchen.

In the main, however, Davies is funny because of the way he speaks. He is always in earnest, and much comedy can be found in his passionate self-regard and the distance between this and the truth: in his claims to superiority over 'Blacks' and 'aliens', for example, or his denunciation of his unhygienic wife keeping her underwear in the vegetable pan, or in describing his treatment at the Luton monastery by 'that bastard monk'. This story (pp. 14–15) is full of marvellous jokes based on his perception of the events. The force of the humour lies in the faint possibility that he might be telling the truth and a monk did tell him to 'piss off', that an Irish monk was aggressive towards him, that he was given a meagre meal, and that he did threaten to report them to their 'mother superior'. It is just possible that the monks were having a bad day and Davies was the last straw – however unlikely it sounds in his telling.

Davies has no understanding of other people and this leads to comic responses when he doesn't follow exactly what is being said. Told that other rooms in the house are 'out of commission' he replies, 'Get away', and that the statue is of Buddha he replies, 'Get on'; given the suggestion that his groaning in the night was due to an unfamiliar bed, he replies, 'There's nothing unfamiliar about me with beds. I slept in beds'; and when Mick pretends to confide in him about Aston, Davies has no idea that the joke is on him:

MICK: Well, what it is, you see, I'm . . . I'm a bit worried about my brother.
DAVIES: Your brother?

MICK: Yes, you see, his trouble is . . .

DAVIES: What?

MICK: Well, it's not a very nice thing to say . . .

DAVIES: (*rising, coming downstage*) Go on now, you
say it.

MICK *looks at him.*

MICK: He doesn't like work.

Pause.

DAVIES: Go on!

MICK: No, he just doesn't like work, that's his trouble.

DAVIES: Is that a fact? (pp. 76–7)

The shift in the mood of the play is marked by the
extent to which Davies stops being funny, and a good
example occurs when he is given another pair of shoes by
Aston which, again, don't fit:

DAVIES: Well, I'll tell you what, they might do . . .
until I get another pair.
Pause.
Where's the laces?

ASTON: No laces.

DAVIES: I can't wear them without laces.

ASTON: I just got the shoes.

DAVIES: Well now, look that puts the lid on it, don't
it? I mean, you couldn't keep these shoes on right
without a pair of laces. (p. 103)

Here, the complaining by Davies is not at all as funny as
in the example considered above. Davies is beginning to
assert his demands under the delusion that he is better off
with the friendship of Mick, and the comic dimension of
the play disappears as the characters become seriously
involved with their individual survival.

There is a degree of comedy in Mick's mischief towards Davies, although this is usually uncanny and double-edged – his main interest is in having Davies evicted. Much of the humour will depend on the personality of the actor playing Mick. The character is at times physically aggressive and vocally abrasive, but this merely highlights the disturbing shifts when he changes into a supposedly friendly ally. Mick is engaged in a protracted game – that is, of baiting Davies – and he is mostly putting on a performance. At times this is funny, and his set-piece monologues are very witty. These speeches (on pp. 45, 46–7 and 53–5) have been compared to the patter of music-hall or radio comedians. There is no need to make the comparison, though, because they have their own distinctive style and structure (discussed in this book on pp. 121–2 below). They are brilliant improvisations intended to confuse and disconcert Davies, but they should always entertain the audience with their comic invention.

Tragic elements

Of all classical forms of drama, tragedy has made the least convincing progress during the twentieth century. This is because Western societies have moved away from the hierarchical structures of old. In the past, tragedy was associated with great figures being destroyed by a fault in their character; with an exploration of the fundamental questions of good and evil; and with the individual being measured against a recognised moral and religious framework. None of these aspects apply to *The Caretaker*, and therefore it would seem inappropriate to consider the play under the criteria applied to classical tragedy. However, theorists have made a case for tragedy in the modern world, in the sense that tragedy cannot be separated from common experience, and the ending of Pinter's play certainly carries a weight and an emotional impact that might reasonably approximate to tragic feeling. Similarly, all three characters in the play are to an extent alienated from society in general, and this, too, broadens the implications of the play – which casts a bleak vision on the life of the time.

Both the dramatist Arthur Miller and the critic Raymond Williams have argued that tragedy changes with the times. A belief in the Delphic oracle, which underpins Sophocles' *Oedipus Rex*, would have been irrelevant to a Jacobean audience watching Shakespeare's *Macbeth*, which acknowledges the divine right of kings. Both beliefs may be seen, in Williams' opinion, as 'a temporary expression of the socially determined culture of the day', and they are no longer held in the twentieth century. Furthermore, it has been argued that Jacobean tragedy (contemporary with late Shakespeare) is not so much concerned with the conduct of the individual as with the society that destroys him: so Middleton's *Women Beware Women*, for example, or Tourneur's *The Revenger's Tragedy* may be regarded as 'tragedies of state' because everybody is implicated and not a single tragic hero. Dramatists in the modern period as varied as Eugene O'Neill, Arthur Miller, Federico Lorca and J. M. Synge have made 'the common man' the subject of tragic plays where the weight of psychological pressures and social expectations oppresses the individual. The common factor in all their serious plays is human suffering. *The Caretaker*, likewise, depicts characters who are deeply affected by factors beyond their control. In their different ways they are all surviving with a degree of courage in the face of circumstances which are, in the main, oppressive.

Davies is certainly in part responsible for his rejection at the end of the play. He has been offered security by Aston, but out of ignorance, selfishness and latent aggression he loses the opportunity and is cast out. It is easy to list the anti-social characteristics of Davies, but there is another side to him which the play fully acknowledges: he is a survivor, and though living on the absolute fringe of society and fearful of all authority he shows determination and spirit. He just might make it to Sidcup for his papers, if weather permits: his courage has helped him in the past:

> DAVIES: Don't know as these shoes'll be much good. It's a hard road, I been down there before. Coming the other way, like. Last time I left there, it was . . . last time . . . getting on a while back . . . the road was bad, the rain was coming down, lucky I didn't die there on the road, but I got here, I kept going, all along . . . yes . . . I kept going all along. (p. 105)

He is hopelessly out of his depth in dealing with Mick, and his aggression towards Aston is unforgivable, but his final pleading is poignant in the extreme:

> DAVIES: But . . . but . . . look . . . listen . . . listen here . . . I mean . . .
> ASTON *turns back to the window.*
> What am I going to do?
> *Pause.*
> What shall I do?
> *Pause.*
> Where am I going to go? (p. 124)

In some ways Davies is reminiscent of Poor Tom, the 'unaccommodated man' of Shakespeare's *King Lear* who is one of society's beggars neglected by the King. The sheer emptiness of Davies' future possibilities has a tragic dimension.

The nameless and faceless authorities that frighten Davies and keep him on the move appear to have damaged Aston. His narrative description of the forced electric shock treatment in hospital, if it is to be believed, is a gruesome account of an 'official' assault on a helpless individual. And Aston has, effectively, been dumped to look after himself. This he attempts to do with immense dignity, but without help from any social services. He has become a recluse, and is as much cut off from society as Davies. The third character, Mick, is better able to look after himself but he is also a disturbed individual. Obsessed and worried about his brother, he expresses his frustration in violence against Davies, and eventually the statue of Buddha. All three are lonely and isolated. They are unable to communicate effectively, however much they try. This lasting impression of the play, of characters isolated in an unsympathetic, violent and unsupportive environment, is a bleak comment on 1950s urban England.

Absurdist elements

In his definitive book *The Theatre of the Absurd* (1961), Martin Esslin included those modern dramatists who take as their starting point a philosophical position: that is, the absence in the modern world of any fundamental or universal law that justifies human life. With the loss of belief in 'God', man's life is regarded as purposeless and meaningless (see pp. 29–31 of this book). Playwrights as varied as Samuel Beckett, Eugene Ionesco and Jean Genet all rejected the naturalistic form as inappropriate to convey their insight into the human condition. Harold Pinter is included in Esslin's book, but it is misleading to associate him closely with the other playwrights because he keeps very much to the tradition of surface naturalism and is committed to psychological realism, which the other Absurdists are not. Where Pinter *can* be regarded in this category, however, is in the existentialist definition of his characters. From another period, John Webster's Flamineo, at the point of death in *The White Devil*, says

> I do not look
> Who went before, nor who shall follow me;
> No, at myself I will begin and end.
>
> (V. v. 259–61)

All Pinter's characters might echo that sentiment. Certainly the three characters in *The Caretaker* are self-oriented, isolated and lonely.

The existentialist dilemma of the characters, Davies, Aston and Mick, is underlined by their lack of positive 'identity' and, to an extent, by their clinging reliance on physical objects. It is significant that we are not introduced to the characters by way of a formal exposition. This would imply from the start that they can be 'known'. In fact we know nothing more about Aston than Davies does. We don't know why he has brought Davies into the house and we don't know if he will build his shed. Likewise we see Mick from the same perspective as Davies: his motives are never explained. Davies, especially, is a remarkable example of confused and uncertain identity. He cannot acknowledge where he was born, he appears to have no family, his very name is uncertain, he has nowhere to live and he has no defined future. The repeated mention of his 'papers' in Sidcup merely emphasises his real predicament

– no papers will alter who or what he is. He is constantly defined in terms of possessions and objects which, cumulatively, expose the limits of his existence: a good pair of shoes, a warm shirt, a knife to cut his bread and a clock ('then I stand a bit of a chance'). Aston, too, is always associated with objects which draw attention to the narrow limits of his life. His room is full of stuff that he has collected for some uncertain future purpose and he goes shopping for more things. He occupies his time fiddling with plugs and a toaster, but nothing gets mended. And if Davies has Sidcup as a possible salvation, and Aston has his garden shed as a future starting point, so Mick has his own fantasy ('I got to think about expanding . . . in all directions'). In fact, all we know about Mick is that he has his own van. The failure of the characters to relate successfully is the ultimate comment that the play makes on their isolated and disconnected lives.

Apparently bizarre or comic business in *The Caretaker* should not be regarded as 'absurd'. It is not meant to expose the meaninglessness of all action (as is the case in the rituals of Vladimir and Estragon in *Waiting for Godot*). Generally it reveals the truth about a relationship on stage. So, when Mick grabs the bag from Davies (Act Two, p. 57), and the object is passed around the trio – snatched by one then another – what might appear a piece of music-hall fun is, in fact, a defining moment in the balance of the relationships. Aston asserts his support of Davies, and Mick, acknowledging this, makes a hasty exit. Again, when Mick questions Aston about the leak in the roof (p. 55) and everybody focuses on the bucket and a solitary drip, the dialogue is stilted, but it is not purely comic. It is Mick's most lengthy attempt to gain a verbal response from his brother.

Characters

A distinctive feature of Pinter's plays is the absence of clear detail about the motivation of the characters and clear detail regarding their past history. They may offer brief hints or talk at great length about their past, but these statements are, somehow, always open to question and doubt. This is certainly true of *The Caretaker*. Mick's complaint about Davies might equally apply to him – 'I can take nothing you say at face value. Every word you speak is open to any number of different interpretations. Most of what you say is lies.' This leads to difficulties for an actor who wishes to build for himself a Stanislavskian background to his character, especially if he wants everything that is spoken to have a cause and needs to know that cause. Equally, it makes character definition a hazardous occupation for the interpretative critic who is also faced with the conflicting evidence. The naturalistic tradition inspired by Ibsen in the nineteenth century brought to the stage characters who were mostly rounded, fully-formed and knowable. Their history is generally clear-cut and we always accept their version of past events in their lives (see p. 13). Pinter disputes this tradition, and has always refused to offer character definitions. The evidence is that when working as a director of his plays or when advising another director he can be very helpful, always referring to the text in hand, but he has clearly stated that these opinions are not for public consumption. His most definitive statement has been that we can know only what the characters say and what they do. Working on this principle, the characters in *The Caretaker* offer a considerable amount of evidence on which to construct a definition of personality.

DAVIES A Pinter play frequently starts off with a good deal of humour but moves towards a sombre and disturbing conclusion. The character of Davies follows this pattern. Most of Act One is very funny indeed, entirely because of how Davies is presented; but the end of the play has a tragic dimension as the implications of Davies' rejection are made to reverberate during his long and hopeless pleading to be allowed back into the room by Aston. It seems that his future will be a continuation as a street beggar, a social reject, with old age threatening his survival. He has lost a possible chance of security.

Pinter has created a remarkable stage personality in his vivid and unsentimental portrayal of the tramp. Davies is an old man who, after years of living on the streets, combines every anti-social characteristic imaginable. He is incapable of holding down a job, or of forming a meaningful relationship; he is aggressive, resentful, whinging and, above all, he stinks. Nevertheless Davies does possess something of a life-force, a defiant energy. This is manifest in his verbal energy, his long speeches and in his physical reaction to any assault on him. Donald Pleasance, the first actor to play Davies, was perfect for the role because he possessed as an actor, according to Pinter, the perfect combination of ferocity, vitality and bewilderment.

As his character unfolds we can see that the key to his days is survival. Part of his make-up after years of living alone involves fantasy and confusion, but his survival depends on fulfilling basic physical needs: a good pair of shoes ('Shoes? It's life and death to me'), a shirt ('a kind of a shirt with stripes') and even, sometimes, 'a piece of soap'. His life is filled with minutiae – a cup of tea, the offer of a bite to eat, 'loosening up' before taking a seat: even the act of sitting down is a priority ('Sit down? Huh . . . I haven't had a good sit down . . . I haven't had a proper sit down . . . Well, I couldn't tell you', and 'Ten minutes off for a tea break in the middle of the night in that place and I couldn't find a seat, not one'). By living in the open – or 'kipping out' as he describes it – his life is limited to the geography of his world – Shepherd's Bush, Acton, Wembley, Watford, the North Circular and the Great West Road – and these places he remembers mostly for their public conveniences and cheap cafés. In this life a three-day hike to Luton on the chance of a free pair of second-hand shoes takes on the status of a heroic quest.

The process of daily survival, as a solitary figure, has over many years caused him to confuse details of his past. It is possible that he had a wife and left her and that he was once in the services 'over there' (presumably before the Second World War). Davies is a Welsh name but there is nothing particularly Welsh in his speech; nor does he speak in a notably cockney idiom, as Max might do in *The Homecoming*. The details of his 'papers' in Sidcup are a mystery, despite their prominence in the play. Davies believes that Sidcup holds the answer to all his problems, especially with the authorities, but he makes no effort to go there and is certainly confused about what these papers might be. Presumably, if he could make it to Luton for a pair of shoes he could make it to Sidcup. But Sidcup, like Moscow for the sisters in Chekhov's *The Three Sisters*, remains somehow unattainable. It is intrinsic to his character that Davies is incapable of giving a straight answer to a serious question, as a form of self-protection, but it is equally likely that he no longer has any answers to give because the past is a haze.

The source of most of the comedy in the play is Davies' belief that he is a person of substance and quality and has 'rights'. His defiant claims that 'I've had dinner with the best' and 'I keep myself up' are preposterous, as is his claim 'nobody's got more rights than I have'. This egotism obviously gets him into trouble. Aston has saved him from a fight caused by his refusal to empty a bucket of rubbish in the café where he was working: 'who was this git to come and give me orders? We got the same standing.' And he clearly feels superior to any foreigner, whoever they may be – 'Poles, Greeks, Blacks, the lot of them, all them aliens'. He deeply resents any suggestion of fault on his part and his outrage is comic both in terms of its expression and its defiance, as for example in his recounting of the monk's refusal to offer him free shoes at the Luton monastery, or challenging Aston when told about his jabbering in his sleep: 'There's nothing unfamiliar about me with beds. I slept in beds. I don't make noises just because I sleep in a bed. I slept in plenty of beds' (p. 31).

Likewise, comedy ensues from his 'choosiness': his rejection of 'suede' shoes because 'it goes off, it creases, it stains for life in five minutes' and his rejection of brown laces for black shoes. He accepts the smoking-jacket but wants to know 'How do you think it looks?' which is a wonderfully irrelevant consideration in his circumstances. His unworldliness involves fear of the gas stove (an interior appliance, and thus one which he is unused to) and a doorbell, which might expose him to an ill-defined outside threat.

His mindless egotism and aggressive instinct are the cause of his undoing in the play. He overreaches himself by turning viciously against Aston in the belief that he is superior – because he, unlike Aston, has never been in a mental hospital ('a nuthouse'). Essentially, however, he is defeated because his self-obsession prevents him from having any understanding of other people. In the play this involves Aston and, more importantly, Mick. He never appreciates what Aston has offered him in the form of a home and a secure occupation. He is more worried that it might involve 'jobs'. And he has no idea at all of the unspoken relationship between the brothers. He is completely unable to follow the process whereby Mick both deludes him into a false sense of security while also using him to try to find out how his brother is getting on. Mick is always a long way ahead of Davies, and controls all the dialogue between them, Davies remaining wholly unaware of Mick's motives:

> DAVIES: I tell you he should go back where he come from!
> MICK: (*turning to look at him*) Come from?
> DAVIES: Yes.
> MICK: Where did he come from?
> DAVIES: Well . . . he . . . he . . .
> MICK: You get a bit out of your depth sometimes, don't you?
> *Pause.*
> (*Rising, briskly*) Well, anyway, as things stand, I don't mind having a go at doing up the place . . .
> DAVIES: That's what I wanted to hear! (p. 114)

In this passage Davies is unconscious of Mick's sensitivity towards Aston's medical history, and is only looking for his own preferment.

The full display of Davies' aggression and unpleasantness is found in his long diatribe against Aston (pp. 106–7).

Here the rhythmic development of his violent instinct is a climactic moment in the play. Everything we have seen and heard about Aston ('I was quite strong then') has hinted at a possible eruption, as if his quietness and stillness were harbouring a latent power. The anticipation in the theatre, during Davies' speech, is of a physical assault:

> DAVIES: . . . You think I'm going to do your dirty work? Haaaaahhhhh! You better think again! You want me to do all the dirty work all up and down them stairs just so I can sleep in this lousy filthy hole every night? Not me, boy. Not for you, boy. You don't know what you're doing half the time. You're up the creek! You're half off!

In the event, however, Aston remains calm and the effect is much more powerful in the theatre than any violent conflict. Davies' speech contains all the reasons why Aston is unmoved during the final sequence of the play, when Davies begs to be allowed back. The fact remains, however, that Davies has imposed his personality so strongly on the audience that his final pleading is poignant.

MICK There is a vivid realism in the presentation of Davies, both in his language and his physical gestures, as he reacts in bewilderment at being offered charity from Aston and suffers violence from Mick. In contrast, both Aston and Mick are more mysterious, because their motives are less obvious. Mick in particular never explains what he is up to and his behaviour is very erratic. Nevertheless, by considering the play in totality it is possible to follow the logic of his behaviour throughout. Everything is determined by his concern for his brother and his jealousy of Davies. This forms the subtext of the play – it motivates everything that Mick does, but it is never mentioned.

The first image on stage in *The Caretaker* is of a silent Mick looking about the room and then staring, expressionless, for thirty seconds – a very long time in theatrical terms. It is a powerful image and establishes Mick firmly in the mind of the audience, who are not going to see him again until the very end of the first act. He leaves the room as soon as he hears the arrival of Aston and Davies. Seeing Mick at the start of the play makes his re-entry less melodramatic – subconsciously the audience will have been expecting to see him again at some time. However, Mick's actions can also be interpreted from a psychological point of view. His brother has had mental treatment and he is a changed man. Mick is greatly concerned about this – and who wouldn't be? – and has established Aston in the house with a view to rehabilitating him. Aston has the job of decorating the place, but isn't doing any decorating; merely collecting bits and pieces which fill the room. What more can Mick do? That is the starting point of the play. The next thing is that Aston brings Davies into the room, and Mick doesn't like this at all. He has the power to eject Davies, but that would alienate him from Aston, so he acts to make Davies unpopular with Aston – which he succeeds in doing. While confusing and deceiving Davies during Acts Two and Three he is constantly asking questions about Aston, which indicates the depth of his concern: ('Who brought you here?', 'Don't you find him friendly, then?', 'What's funny about him?').

Working-class characters on the English stage have rarely been dignified with much intelligence. Traditionally they have often been staged for comedy, from a patronising point of view. Or, alternatively, the 'poor' have been granted a worthy honesty, which is equally patronising. Mick, however, like Max, Lenny and Teddy in *The Homecoming*, is very bright indeed. His intelligence is evident in his verbal flexibility and invention. He behaves erratically and he is deeply conscious of the mental history of his brother, but although he is clearly frustrated there is no suggestion that he is mentally disturbed himself. With Davies he is generally putting on a performance, which he can do with ease, but when confronted by Aston the depth of his relationship renders him inarticulate. In the film of *The Caretaker* there is a scene included of the two brothers standing silently looking into the pond in the garden. The image communicates rather more than can be achieved on the stage: a fundamental fraternal love which does not involve speech. On p. 120, when Aston returns to the room, the stage direction underlines this:

> ASTON *comes in. He closes the door, moves into the room and faces* MICK. *They look at each other. Both are smiling, faintly.*
> MICK: (*beginning to speak to* ASTON) Look . . . uh . . .
> *He stops, goes to the door and exits.*

When Mick describes his dream penthouse and Davies asks, 'Who would live there?' the answer is, 'I would. My brother and me.' This is part of Mick's dream, and it is the key to Mick's character.

ASTON Of the three characters in the play, Aston offers the longest, fullest commentary on his own past, during his monologue at the close of Act Two. He describes his experience of electric shock treatment in such graphic detail as to make it sound more like torture than therapy, and he the victim of a callous authority rather than a patient undergoing helpful treatment in order that he could 'go out . . . and live like the others'. His story is delivered hesitantly, as if he is trying to reconstruct his experience for the first time. What he remembers begins 'years ago now' when he used to visit the café nearby and 'talk about things'. This habit of talking a lot, to older men, he carried into the workplace, which he says was a factory and where he was employed on a manufacturing line ('standing there'). He remembers having moments of clear insight – 'kind of hallucinations' – when 'I used to get the feeling I could see things . . . very clearly.' He believes that this condition brought about his removal to a hospital where he was examined and, with the written permission of his mother, given electric shock treatment. As Aston describes the experience it appears that, as a much younger and stronger man, he fought against the medical staff but was overpowered. Following the treatment he was left unable to organise his thoughts, couldn't hear properly and stopped talking to people. He lived with his mother and brother as a recluse.

If this is true, it helps make sense of what we see of Aston in the play. By implication it might be assumed that Mick, the younger brother, in attempting to rehabilitate Aston, has provided him with a place to live and an occupation – the decorating of the house. Aston understands this and has his own plan, which means beginning by building a work-shed in the garden. The room is filled with objects which have probably been brought in by Aston for future use, either from other rooms or from shops. His proposed purchase of a jigsaw fits into this pattern of preparation. His mending of the leak in the roof suggests a further development in his progress, following his disclosure about his past to Davies.

His behaviour in the play is consistent with that of someone who has lost faith with family (who conspired with the medical authorities) and society (who betrayed him in the first place), but is beginning to make some kind of recovery. His treatment of Davies is exceptional. Possibly he recognises someone worse off than himself, and gains some comfort from another possession. His gestures of hospitality are altogether magnanimous and his forbearance in the company of an unpleasant room-mate quite amazing. His speech is most reticent, especially in contrast to that of Davies and Mick, and his introversion in a play of only three characters could make him an oddity; however, in performance, the character can take on a very sympathetic quality, as Robert Shaw succeeded in doing in the film version.

The play offers no reason as to why Aston should have brought Davies into his room, but having done so their relationship unfolds very clearly up to the point where Davies is rejected. Everything prepares an audience to expect a violent crisis in Act Three, with Aston exploding in reaction to Davies' vicious outburst against him. Aston has suggested that he used to be a very powerful man, and Davies' long speech threatening him with a return to the mental institution positively invites a physical response. However, Aston's response is infinitely more dignified and theatrically compelling:

> I . . . I think it's about time you found somewhere else. I don't think we're hitting it off.

Dramatic Structure

The structure of the play, in three Acts, relies on the basic naturalistic rules of time, place and action. Everything takes place in one room, very clearly described and placed. The place names make West London the setting, but Mick widens this to nearer Hackney in his monologue. Working-class urban North London in the late 1950s is the place. The film of *The Caretaker* gives a clear picture of this world and insists on the relevance of the 'outside' by including scenes of the tramp in the street, of Mick in his van, and of the brothers in the garden – so not everything takes place in a vacuum, disputing the idea that the outside world doesn't intrude in a Pinter play.

Three characters, very differently defined by their gestures and language, are the sole matter for attention, and the action follows the consequences of Davies being introduced to the room. The play is meticulously crafted, so that while attention is always held at each moment of action by the relationship/s on stage, there is an inevitability about the progression, and each act ends on a moment of high theatrical tension.

The naturalistic detail of the setting is complemented by the stage business of the characters, which is usually connected with the objects in the room. For example, during the first scene Aston says very little indeed compared to Davies, but he is constantly engaged, slowly, in physical action. This stage business can be choreographed as follows: Aston looks for a chair and places it for Davies to sit on. He sits on the bed and begins to roll himself a cigarette, which he then lights. He offers tobacco to Davies who fills his pipe. He crosses the room to collect an electric toaster and, returning to his bed, he starts to unscrew the plug. He then crosses to the plug box to get another plug which he starts to fix to the toaster. He then searches under his bed for a pair of shoes which he offers to the tramp, and continues attending to the toaster. He rises to lift the sack at the window so that Davies can see the back garden. With Davies' help he shifts some of the objects in order to bring out a spare bed. He finds a sheet and pillow and puts them on the bed. He then begins to roll another cigarette. He sorts out five shillings and offers them to Davies, and starts again to poke the plug with a screwdriver. All this business, seemingly inconsequential, is dramatically significant. It helps to present Aston's character, and heightens the focus and concentration on Davies.

The play explores the changing relationships of Aston and Davies and Mick and Davies in a series of dualogues. Virtually all of the dialogue is carried out within these relationships, but the vital underlying and determining relationship is that between the brothers Aston and Mick. The most poignant and ironic fact of the play is that they are virtually incapable of verbal communication, and never converse. However, it is their relationship that provides much of the subtext that operates in the dualogues of Acts Two and Three. Most of Act One provides a vivid demonstration of the character of Davies the tramp, and although Mick cannot be said to be directly relevant to the actual dialogue of Act One, his presence on stage at the start of the play imposes a subconscious 'note' in the mind of the audience.

Mick's ensuing relationship with Davies in Acts Two and Three has Aston as the subtextual motive. Frequently he is, although absent from the stage, the subject of the dialogue between Mick and Davies. But it is the reality of the relationship between the brothers that motivates Mick's shifting verbal strategies. Mick is both assessing Davies, planning how to get rid of him, but always seeking as much information as he can about his brother – which shows the extent of his concern. Davies is never able to see through Mick's thought-processes and remains wholly ignorant of his strategies. Consequently he is deluded into a very false sense that his future security rests more with Mick than with Aston. Act Three shows the increase in Davies' alienation from Aston, his growing viciousness and aggression, and the fulfilment of Mick's intention that all this will lead to the tramp's expulsion – not by him directly, but by Aston.

Language

The most distinctive and original feature of *The Caretaker* is its language. Not only does Pinter make the ungrammatical and hesitant speech of Davies dramatically vivid, but he shows how people *use* language for personal advantage. So two aspects of the play's language are most relevant: the actual idiom and style of speech of the working-class characters, and the purpose to which language is applied. Although it became something of a cliché to talk of plays of the 1950s and 1960s being concerned with 'lack of communication', it can be seen that throughout *The Caretaker* the characters are very rarely on the same wavelength when it comes to dialogue; they each have different motives. Davies has the greatest difficulty understanding what is being said to him and is frustrated by his own linguistic inadequacy ('But you don't understand my meaning!' could be his watchword). The importance of language in the play, as it defines the identities of the characters and their inability to relate, is underlined by the final stage direction – *Long silence*.

Curtain. – which shows that there is nothing left to be said between them.

In *The Caretaker* Pinter signals a marked departure from the traditional notion that stage characters should be articulate and should converse with consideration and understanding of each other. What he presents is a revealing awareness of how people, especially less-educated people, actually speak. What might appear to be an absurd sequence of non sequiturs can be, in reality, a psychologically accurate depiction of mental processes. In the following sequence, for example, everything follows from what has gone before:

ASTON: You've got to have a good pair of shoes.
DAVIES: Shoes? It's life and death to me. I had to go all the way to Luton in these.
ASTON: What happened when you got there, then?
Pause.
DAVIES: I used to know a bootmaker in Acton. He was a good mate to me.
Pause.
You know what that bastard monk said to me?
Pause.
How many more Blacks you got around here then?
ASTON: What?
DAVIES: You got any more Blacks around here?
ASTON: (*holding out the shoes*) See if these are any good. (p. 13)

Three lines of conversation are concerning Davies, all at the same time. The subject is shoes. Davies is in need of some better shoes than the sandals he is wearing. He has mentioned being let down by a monastery in Luton which was reputed to provide shoes. Aston is trying to follow the story, point by point, but Davies' mind jumps from 'shoes' to 'a bootmaker in Acton', then back to the monks in Luton, then further back to the black neighbours that have been mentioned before. Aston concentrates on the shoes all the time. The sequence is entirely realistic on a psychological level: Aston trying to be helpful, and Davies partly keeping up with his story but also showing his confusion about his new surroundings.

A consistent feature of Davies' personality, reflected in his language, is his inability or refusal to answer any direct question – from either Aston or Mick (see the examples on p. 17, 'would you like to sleep here?'; p. 26, 'How long's he had them?'; p. 35, 'You Welsh?' and 'Where were you born?'; p. 43, 'What's your name?'). This is natural to him after a lifetime of evasive self-defence. His constant repetition, failure to complete sentences and evasiveness become stylised to a high degree. At times this can be both funny and desperately poignant when the audience can see the problem that he is confronted with. For example, when offered the job of caretaker, the opportunity is there for security, a bed, warmth and relative comfort; but, and it is a big but for Davies, it might involve work. It takes him some time to actually mention the dreaded word – 'jobs'. The sequence of dialogue is far removed from conventional stage 'conversation', but it is entirely realistic and true to the characters:

ASTON: How do you feel about being one, then?
DAVIES: Well, I reckon . . . Well, I'd have to know . . . you know . . .
ASTON: What sort of . . .
DAVIES: Yes, what sort of . . . you know . . .

Pause.
ASTON: Well, I mean . . .
DAVIES: I mean, I'd have to . . . I'd have to . . .
ASTON: Well, I could tell you . . .
DAVIES: That's . . . that's it . . . you see . . . you get my
  meaning?
ASTON: When the time comes . . .
DAVIES: I mean, that's what I'm getting at, you see . . .
ASTON: More or less exactly what you . . .
DAVIES: You see, what I mean to say . . . what I'm
  getting at is . . . I mean, what sort of jobs . . .
  (pp. 66–7)

Towards the end of the play Davies says to Mick that
Aston has been ignoring him and not talking to him, but it
is clear that whenever Aston *has* tried to start a conversation it is Davies who fails to respond. This can be seen on
pp. 20–1, when he is shown the statue of Buddha; on p. 23,
when Aston mentions his preference for drinking Guinness
out of a thin glass; on pp. 33–4, when Aston talks firstly
about his tools and then about a woman propositioning
him in a café; and on pp. 62–3 when he considers the decorating of the house. On each occasion Davies shows no
interest in developing the subject. On one level, for those
readers or listeners who are used to a sequential dialogue,
these breakdowns in logical progression might seem odd –
in particular, they can make Aston appear odd – but in fact
they reflect a real personal situation, where Davies is
incapable of responding in a friendly or helpful way.

The relationship between Davies and Mick shows Mick
to be the dominant figure. He begins by terrifying the
tramp with a combination of physical and verbal assault.
Here Mick uses language as a weapon:

MICK: What's your name?
DAVIES: (*shifting, about to rise*) Now look here!
MICK: What?
DAVIES: Jenkins!
MICK: Jen . . . kins.

> DAVIES *makes a sudden move to rise. A violent*
> *bellow from* MICK *sends him back.*
> (*A shout*) Sleep here last night?

DAVIES: Yes . . .
MICK: (*continuing at great pace*) How'd you sleep?
   (p. 48)

Mick is genuinely angry at the intrusion of Davies, and he has an underlying motive of removing him, but he is also interested in how Aston is progressing. His questions, therefore, are double-edged. He knows full well that Aston brought Davies to the room, but he wants to know why:

DAVIES: I was brought here!
   Pause.
MICK: Pardon?
DAVIES: I was brought here! I was brought here!
MICK: Brought here? Who brought you here?
DAVIES: Man who lives here . . . he . . .
   Pause.
MICK: Fibber. (p. 51)

He could evict Davies at any time, but that might risk alienating his brother, so he deceives the tramp into a false sense of security. Davies never has any idea of the feeling that exists between the brothers and he has no perception of how Mick is manipulating him. In the following sequence the two are far apart. Mick is self-conscious about his brother's past illness and sensitive to the term 'funny' (meaning 'strange'), but he keeps control and changes tack. Davies doesn't notice:

DAVIES: Well . . . he's a funny bloke, your brother.

MICK: What?

DAVIES: I was saying, he's . . . he's a bit of a funny bloke, your brother.

MICK *stares at him.*

MICK: Funny? Why?

DAVIES: Well . . . he's funny . . .

MICK: What's funny about him?

Pause.

DAVIES: Not liking work.

MICK: What's funny about that?

DAVIES: Nothing.

Pause.

MICK: I don't call it funny.

DAVIES: Nor me.

MICK: You don't want to start getting hypercritical.

DAVIES: No, no, I wasn't that, I wasn't . . . I was only saying . . .

MICK: Don't get too glib.

DAVIES: Look, all I meant was –

MICK: Cut it! (*Briskly*) Look! I got a proposition to make to you. (pp. 79–80)

All three characters are given long set-speeches, or monologues. These reflect intimately on the speaker, but never progress into a conversation. They make different demands on the actors because of their different form, but Mick's are the most stylised and surreal. At the beginning of Act Two he bamboozles Davies with three brilliant improvisations. These begin, 'You remind me of my uncle's brother' (p. 45); 'You know, believe it or not, you've got a funny kind of resemblance to a bloke I once knew in Shoreditch' (p. 46); and 'You're stinking the place out' (p. 53). Each speech follows a similar structure and ends with a question directed at Davies pertaining to the immediate situation ('I hope you slept well last night', for example). They establish Mick as the dominating force in the room (and the theatre). Although Mick involves Davies in the speeches ('Very much your build' and 'Dead spit of you he was'), they are essentially jazz-like improvisations on various themes drawn from Mick's imagination. The first plays with the notion of an uncle's brother being a bit of an athlete, the two ideas being played off against each other. The second revolves around 'a bloke I once knew' and the topography of North and West London. The wit involved in Pinter's writing relates to the possibilities involved. All the places really exist and Putney *is* close to Fulham ('Even if they weren't born in Putney they were born in Fulham'). The speeches move to the limits of imaginative invention, before Mick turns the fun into a serious question, putting Davies at a disadvantage:

> MICK: . . . Of course we'd need a signed declaration
> from your personal medical attendant as assurance
> that you possess the requisite fitness to carry the can,
> won't we? Who do you bank with?
> *Pause.*
> Who do you bank with? (pp. 54–5)

When Mick fantasises about his possible penthouse (pp. 96–7) the vision is not absurd. It may be abstracted from a world of modern advertising but it indicates the vividness of Mick's imagination and underlines the sadness of his life.

If Mick's monologues are imaginative set-pieces, the longer speeches of Davies tend to be emotional out-pourings revolving around a single word or idea. Their dramatic force comes from the driving rhythm and intensity of feeling of the speaker, though often the subject is trivial and limited. The repetition of a single word at the centre of Davies' speeches is often their keynote, as can be seen by reference to the following: buckets (p. 5), rights (p. 6), soap (p. 12), shoes (p. 15), stamps (p. 25), shirts (p. 64), names and cards (p. 68), clock (p. 99) and beds (pp. 121–2). In every case the item is made a matter of extreme personal importance, so Davies is always really talking about himself and rarely do his passionate declarations develop into a dialogue of significance.

Aston has his long autobiographical speech at the end of Act Two. It certainly makes an effective climax to the act, and is powerful because of its content and the effort that it costs the speaker. Its theatricality is emphasised by the '*gradual, protracted and unobtrusive*' fade-down of light. As a narrative it is compelling because of the focus on being treated in a mental hospital and the awfulness involved. It might be worth considering the truthfulness of the story – doubt has been cast on the likelihood of such violence being inflicted in a state hospital in the 1950s – but the story is clearly a reflection of Aston's perception of events, and who knows what was going on in his mind at the time he was in hospital? Why did his mother consent to the operation? The speech is always effective because Aston has been a mysterious figure for two Acts and the audience wants to know about him. The play does not offer any contradictory information regarding his past. The speech adds another dimension to the theme of 'identity' and the play's recognition that 'knowing' other people is virtually impossible.

The Caretaker: In Conclusion

The Caretaker has many familiar elements of a conventional naturalistic play: a single set reflecting the period when the play was written; three acts, each moving to a very theatrical climax; even a plot, with Davies intruding between two brothers, being deceived by Mick, and being evicted. However, the play has always been regarded as remarkable because of the central role of Davies the tramp. Never in the English theatre has such a lowly social figure taken centre stage and been realised with such vivid perception. The situation of Davies being welcomed in by Aston and thus provoking the jealous resentment of Mick gives rise to contrasting emotions. The character of Davies is shown by turns to be very funny and very selfish, aggressive and unsympathetic. The brothers have a poignant relationship – they can barely talk to each other, but the family tie proves strong and lasting.

The play signals a marked departure from the idea that characters on stage should be articulate and able to converse with some degree of sympathy and understanding. Davies speaks with vigour and passion but without any of the grammatical 'correctness' that was usual on the West End stage at the time. His speech is, nevertheless, an extremely accurate reflection of the rhythms, the vocabulary and the confusion of a man unused to social relationships. In sharp contrast, Mick uses langauge in a highly stylised manner, which is intended to confuse and control Davies.

Written at a time when the English theatre was becoming preoccupied with examining 'the state of the nation', *The Caretaker* might be seen as presenting a very bleak vision of the isolation of mid-century urban man. In the theatre, however, the play is gripping because of the powerful interplay of characters – an almost old-fashioned concept in the rapidly changing theatrical scene of the 1960s.

Textual Notes

Act One

vii *A room* – for comment on the significance of 'the room' in early Pinter, see pp. 3–6.

– *statue of Buddha* – Buddha, or 'the Enlightened One', is the name given to Siddharta Guatama, the Indian founder of Buddhism. Among other things, the Buddha represents compassion, which makes the statue an appropriate property for Aston.

– *electrolux* – a vacuum cleaner.

1 *silence for thirty seconds* – this long silence at the start of the play imposes the image of Mick firmly in the mind of the audience, who thereafter will – perhaps unconsciously – be expecting his reappearance. From a psychological point of view, although an audience could not know this at the time, the image reflects the hopelessness of Mick's relationship with Aston.

– *shambling, breathing heavily* – throughout the play Davies is shown through his physical gestures and exclamations to be unfamiliar with both the indoors and personal company.

– *vest, no shirt* – the fact that Davies is a tramp should be obvious from his appearance. Much comedy in the play derives from his clothes and shoes.

2 Poles, Greeks, Blacks, the lot of them – Davies considers all 'foreigners' and 'aliens' as inferior to himself.

– come at me – attacked me.

3 done in – killed.

– knocked off – stolen.

– Great West Road – the main road leading from London to the west and south-west of England in the 1950s. Davies constantly refers to places by name, which helps to define his style of life – always travelling from one place to another. All the town names in the play are real places in the vicinity of London.

4 You wouldn't grumble – a colloquial expression indicating agreement.

– filthy skate – skate is a fish, but here the term is simply one of abuse.

– I've had dinner with the best – I've eaten with very good company in my time. Davies has delusions of self-importance which are more comic than pathetic in the early part of the play.

– toe-rags – a term of abuse.

– on the road – living outdoors.

– I keep myself up – respectable (another delusion).

5 handy – strong, able to look after oneself in a fight.

– a few attacks – if Davies is referring to recent illness there is no further mention of it in the play.

- *He crosses down right* – for comment on Aston's movement, see this book, p. 114.
- this git – a dismissive, abusive term for a person.
- same standing – same status: again Davies is preoccupied with his sense of self-importance.
6 guvnor – governor, colloquial for employer.
- give me the bullet – gave me the sack, dismissed me.
- I got my rights – another delusion.
7 a few bob – a few shillings, in old money; a colloquial term which in this context means quite a lot of money.
8 kipping out – sleeping in the open air.
9 out of commission – not in use.
10 caff – café.
12 bastards at the monastery – there is much comedy in this sequence where Davies forcefully abuses monks, traditionally the mildest of men.
- the convenience – public lavatory.
- slipped me – gave me (furtively).
14 en I? – aren't I?
15 mother superior – a good joke (on Pinter's part, not Davies'). A mother superior is in charge of a convent of nuns, not a monastery.
- Irish hooligan – to refer to a monk as a hooligan is purely comic.
- Watford, North Circular, Hendon – these landmarks are easily found on a map of North London.
- they're gone – worn out.
- flog me – sell me.
- some suede – suede shoes.
16 Not much cop – not very good.
- fixed up . . . sorted out – find yourself a permanent job.

18 a shed – Aston's shed is often compared with
   Davies' papers in Sidcup as wishful thinking on
   both their parts.

23 *five shillings* – although this equates to only 25p in
   decimal currency it would have been a very
   generous sum in 1960.

23 Guinness . . . thick mug . . . thin glass – some
   people are very choosy about what kind of glass
   they drink out of. The Irish stout Guinness is
   traditionally poured into a glass without a handle.
   Aston's attempt at conversation gets nowhere.

 – Sidcup – Davies' 'papers' in Sidcup have become a
   famous detail of modern drama.

25 insurance card – National Insurance payments are
   obligatory for all employees and contribute towards
   benefits in the event of the unemployment or
   sickness, and towards a pension. Proof of payment
   used to be stamps on a card.

 – the nick – prison.

 – the nigs – a generalised term of abuse (from
   'niggers').

26 the war – most probably the Second World War
   (1939–45).

28 Dead out – Davies confirms that he slept well.

35 Welsh, are you? – both Jenkins and Davies are
   common Welsh names.

42 What's the game? – What are you up to?

Act Two

44 I'm awfully glad. It's awfully nice to meet you. –
   the repetition of 'awfully' gives the line a false
   refinement (in marked contrast to Mick's physical

violence), introducing Mick's wordplay which is intended to confuse and bewilder Davies.

45 You remind me . . . – for comment on Mick's monologues in this scenes see this book, p. 121.

– penchant – a fondness.

46 Shoreditch, Aldgate, Camden Town, Finsbury Park, Putney, Fulham . . . – all areas of suburban London, well known to inhabitants of London generally. There is considerable wit in Pinter's juxtaposition of the real place-names and bus numbers in this speech, but some of this may be lost on audiences and readers who are unfamiliar with the territory.

– a pitch – a place where a market trader might keep his barrow or stall.

47 Dead spit – an absolute lookalike (from 'spitting image').

49 (*Quietly*) Choosy. – part of Mick's verbal assault on Davies involves this varying of pitch: he 'bellows' and then goes quiet.

52 perky – cheeky, impudent.

53 seven quid – seven pounds.

– exclusive – not including furniture or running costs, such as heat or light.

– Rateable value – properties are given a rateable value by local authorities according to their size and value; rates contribute to local services such as street lighting, cleaning and rubbish collecting.

54 loitering with intent – hanging around with the intention of committing a crime.

– On the other, if you prefer . . . – Mick's inventiveness becomes increasingly surreal during this speech. See this book, p. 121.

– comprehensive indemnity against . . . – Mick lists

all the possible, and impossible, causes of damage to the property which would be covered by insurance.

55 carry the can – take responsibility for.

58 Scrub it – stop it.

59 You're knocking at the door . . . – colloquial expression implying that Davies is wasting his time.

64 *smoking-jacket* – a sophisticated jacket, often made of silk or velvet, associated with upper-class people but rarely worn these days.

68 they'd have me in – put me in prison. Davies' fear is probably unjustified.

71 I was just doing some spring cleaning – this speech is patently untrue.

72 spiky – difficult, awkward.

80 Cut it! – Mick has been using Davies to find out all he can about his brother, but when Davies calls him 'funny' (which can mean mentally disturbed) it touches Mick deeply. The insincerity of his questioning is underlined by this swift change of direction.

81 the services – the armed services such as the army.

82 deeds – documents that prove ownership of property.

83 references – names of people who can guarantee Davies' suitability for employment. Obviously Mick is covering himself and preparing a trap for Davies, who is most unlikely to be able to produce a reference or testimonial.

88 *During* ASTON's *speech the room grows darker* – this is a rare occasion in the play when a technical lighting change is used to heighten the dramatic effect of the language.

89 hallucinations – the experience of seeing things that do not exist.

90 a minor – someone who is under-age.

91 laid one of them out – knocked one of them out.

Act Three

96 penthouse – a luxurious top-floor apartment.

97 clobber – rubbish.

– tuppence – two pence (old money).

100 give him a mouthful – tell him firmly what he thinks.

101 Listen to some Tchaikovsky – the allusion to the Russian classical composer shows the complete distance between the two characters. It is a cynical comment from Mick, who is in the process of manipulating Davies.

106 They took you in – into the mental hospital.
off your nut – crazy.

107 a creamer – a mad person.

– up the creek, half off – insane.

– nuthouse – mental hospital.

108 I don't think we're hitting it off – not getting on very well: this devastating understatement is much more dramatically effective than any act of violence that might have been carried out by Aston.

113 en he . . . en't – hasn't he? isn't it?
sitting tenant – the person who is in residence.

117 nutty – mentally ill.

119 half a dollar, half a crown – two shillings and sixpence in old money (twelve and a half pence in decimal currency).

120 chuck it in – stop bothering or worrying about it.

The Homecoming

Synopsis

Although the list of characters in the published text of *The Homecoming* lists only their sex and age, as always in the case of Harold Pinter (see pp. 8–9), it is useful to know the family relationships when reading a synopsis. Max, a retired butcher (aged seventy), lives with his brother Sam (aged sixty-three) and two of his sons – Lenny (aged early thirties) and Joey (aged middle twenties). They are visited by Max's eldest son Teddy (aged middle thirties) and his wife Ruth (aged early thirties).

The play takes place in a large room of an old house in North London.

ACT ONE Lenny is sitting on a sofa ticking off horses in a newspaper. Max enters looking for a pair of scissors and they have an acrimonious exchange. Max remembers when he and a friend called MacGregor used to make a big impression in the West End of London as hard men, and he recalls his days on the racecourse when he used to have a gift for recognising the best horses. Lenny changes the subject by complaining about Max's poor cooking. Sam enters in his chauffeur's uniform. He has driven a wealthy American to Heathrow Airport and been given a box of cigars. He claims to be the most popular of the firm's chauffeurs. Max responds by asking why he never got married. Sam says there is still time, and recalls how he used to escort Jessie, Max's wife, in the old days when Max was busy. Joey enters. He has been training as a boxer in the gym. He and Sam say they are hungry, expecting Max to provide dinner. He reacts furiously. Sam reminds Max that he was trusted in the past with escorting Jessie – something Max would never have allowed MacGregor (now dead) to do. Max threatens Sam with eviction when he stops working. The scene ends in blackout.

When the lights come up it is night. Teddy and Ruth are standing at the threshold of the room with suitcases. Teddy has brought his wife of six years to meet his family. They have come from America where Teddy is a professor of philosophy. Teddy is anxious not to wake the sleeping family. He encourages Ruth to go to bed, saying that she needs some rest. She asks if he really wants to stay and suddenly says she wants to go for a walk to 'have a breath of air'. Teddy is left standing alone when Lenny enters from his downstairs room. Lenny complains of not being able to sleep. Teddy goes upstairs to bed. Lenny lights a cigarette and sits, waiting. Ruth returns and Lenny begins to question her. She explains that she is Teddy's wife and that they are on a visit to Europe and have been to Italy. Lenny engages in a series of speeches designed to impress Ruth, including two long stories where he describes his violent assault on women who have been unreasonable to him. Finally he approaches Ruth and attempts to remove her glass of water. Ruth is unmoved by any of Lenny's tactics and reverses the proceedings, saying, 'If you take the glass . . . I'll take you.' Lenny is unnerved and accuses her of making some kind of proposal. She leaves him and goes upstairs. Max is wakened by Lenny's shouting and comes downstairs asking what the matter is. Lenny refuses to answer and, when Max persists, he demands to know the details of his own conception ('What was it like? What was the background to it?') Max spits at him and leaves. The scene ends in blackout.

In the morning Joey is seen shadow-boxing in front of a mirror. Max enters complaining that he has been driven out of the kitchen by the noise of Sam washing up the breakfast dishes. He calls Sam into the room and accuses him of being resentful. Teddy and Ruth come downstairs wearing dressing-gowns. When Max sees them for the first time he accuses Teddy of bringing a whore into the house and demands that Joey chuck them out. Joey calls him 'an old man'. Max hits Joey with all his might and begins to collapse with the effort; he then hits Sam with his stick when Sam comes to help him. Getting to his feet, Max asks Ruth how many children she has (three), and, turning to Teddy, he asks for a cuddle and kiss. Teddy faces him and responds, 'Come on, Dad. I'm ready for the cuddle.'

ACT TWO It is afternoon and the family are having a coffee after lunch. Max reminisces about his wife, Jessie, 'the backbone to this family', who had 'a will of iron, a heart of gold and a mind'. He is then riled by Sam's not going to work, and bemoans how much he has had to work to bring up his family. He regrets not having been to Teddy's wedding and expresses his delight at the success of the married couple. Lenny begins to question Teddy on matters of philosophy, but Teddy refuses to be drawn. Ruth diverts attention to herself and her physical presence. She says that she was born nearby, but left for America, which she describes as 'all rock. And sand'.

Max, Lenny and Joey exit. Teddy is left alone with Ruth. He is anxious to return to America but she shows no enthusiasm. Teddy leaves to pack. Lenny enters and sits by Ruth. She tells him of her past when she was 'a photographic model for the body'. Teddy returns with the suitcases expecting to leave with Ruth, but Lenny puts on a record of slow jazz and asks her for a dance. When Max and Joey return, Lenny is kissing Ruth – while Teddy stands by with Ruth's coat. Joey takes Ruth from Lenny, sits with her on the sofa and embraces her. Max notices that Teddy is ready to leave and wishes him well. Ruth suddenly pushes Joey away, stands up and demands something to eat from Joey and something to drink from Lenny. Lenny pours drinks all round. Ruth asks Teddy if the family have read his critical works and he replies that they wouldn't understand them because the family lack 'intellectual equilibrium'. The scene ends in blackout.

In the evening Teddy is sitting with Sam, who confides that he was always his favourite, and his mother's favourite, of all the sons. Lenny enters, goes to the sideboard and discovers that a cheese roll that he has made has disappeared. Teddy says that he has eaten it. This provokes a lengthy accusation from Lenny that Teddy has let the family down by withdrawing to America and becoming 'A bit sulky. A bit inner'. Joey comes downstairs and Lenny asks him how he has got on with Ruth. Joey says that he didn't get 'all the way'. Lenny tells Teddy that his wife is a tease. Max and Sam enter and hear what's been going on between Joey and Ruth. Max suggests that the family asks Ruth to stay with them and each could contribute to her upkeep. Lenny argues that it would be less expensive if he set her up as a prostitute: Teddy could act as their representative in America, supplying clients.

When Ruth comes downstairs Teddy puts the family's proposition to her. She makes stringent demands as to the conditions she would expect if she were to agree to the offer, which Max and Lenny accept. Sam steps forward and declares 'MacGregor had Jessie in the back of my cab as I drove them along' and then collapses. The family are unconcerned about this collapse. Teddy takes his leave. Ruth sits, relaxed. Joey kneels before her and puts his head in her lap. Max falls on his knees by the side of her chair and Lenny stands, watching.

The Play

Reading a synopsis of *The Homecoming* can be both shocking and misleading. It is shocking for what appears to be a wholesale assault on traditional family values. It is misleading, as indeed a reading of the full play can be, because the dimension of live performance is missing. In the theatre the play progresses from a realistic introduction to the domestic setting and the family group to a conclusion which involves a stage picture of Ruth in a tableau surrounded by Joey (with his head in her lap), Max (kneeling) and Lenny (watching). This is both surreal and poetic. A disturbing shift occurs as the audience is taken over by what is happening on stage, and is held in hypnotic awe.

The events of the play are as frightful and as daring as a playwright could go in 1965. An aged father verbally abuses a son and brother; spits at one son and physically assaults another. A brother attempts to seduce his brother's wife on first meeting her. A daughter-in-law is greeted by her father as 'a smelly scrubber' and 'a stinking pox-ridden slut'. A husband proposes to his wife that she sets up as a prostitute and lives with his family in order to service them as well. She agrees to the offer. This all seems incredible and obscene. However, the final image of the seated woman, relaxed and centre stage, surrounded by a group of needy men, is very powerful and offers many possible interpretations – not least the question of what will happen next. Also, the play presents archetypes of family relationships with such vivid intensity that an audience is made to react beyond the purely rational level. We cannot simply conclude 'this wouldn't happen'. The play does happen and we become involved with the characters. We are forced to respond.

More than ever in this play Pinter refuses to offer explanations and motivations. He establishes a situation – the arrival of Teddy and Ruth into the family home – and follows the consequences scene by scene. All the subsequent action is determined by the psychological motives of the characters. In the theatre an audience is held by each confrontation as it happens, and is unlikely to ask too many questions about motivation while the play is in performance. But the play is very provocative and if we are shown the tip of the iceberg in the form of dialogue between Lenny and Max, or Teddy and Ruth, we are inclined to want to know more of what is below the surface: what is the background or the subtext to these exchanges?

All of the many commentators on the play eventually confront the central questions. Why does Ruth agree to leave her comfortable family in America, and why does Teddy do nothing to stop her? The play is rich in ambiguity and is intrinsically puzzling, so finally the answers cannot be known for certain. Part of the richness of the play, and what creates its poetic quality, is precisely this area of uncertainty. Without attempting to fix a *meaning* to the play, therefore, it should be possible to ask how these central questions are made dramatically interesting. Initially, this requires an examination of the family and the presentation of Ruth.

The family

The Homecoming presents us with a family, and a very particular family. All the characters of the play belong to one family and we are not concerned with anybody else except Jessie, the dead mother, and MacGregor – also dead, but uncomfortably close to this family. In the vast catalogue of drama, stretching back to ancient Greek theatre, the family unit has taken a central role, which is hardly surprising given that it reflects the essential human condition, the fundamental social group. Agamemnon is killed by Clytemnestra because he sacrificed their daughter. Medea kills her children because she has been betrayed by her husband. Oedipus kills his father and marries his mother, thereby establishing the benchmark for what is absolutely taboo in family relationships. In Shakespeare's *King Lear* the nature of good and evil is explored through the experience of two families, fathers and children, sons and daughters. Nearer our time the greatest dramatists have been obsessed with the ambivalent nature of family life – Chekhov, Strindberg and O'Neill are obvious examples. Pinter's *The Homecoming* makes a powerful contribution to this catalogue of family plays because it examines archetypal relationships with ruthless objectivity, devoid of any moral agenda.

Some early reviewers of *The Homecoming* were completely put off by what they dismissed as an ugly, brutal, foul-mouthed bunch living in a slum. Most reviews were at least equivocal, recognising the brilliance of the writing but unhappy with the content. So 'this tremendous play' is also 'horrible' and 'repellent'; it is 'extremely funny and deeply unnerving'; it 'revolts but fascinates'. It is easy to see how the first audiences in Cardiff and Brighton, entirely middle-class and happy with Gilbert and Sullivan, were shocked by this play. The language and behaviour are disturbing. In the years since it was written, in 1965, audiences have tended to be less shocked, more intrigued and far more open to the humour in the play. However, from the beginning another perspective was offered. Paul Rogers, the actor who first played Max, has said 'This is a very lovely family' and Pinter calls them 'a fine old mob'. Teddy, in the play, says, 'They're very warm people, really. Very warm. They're my family. They're not ogres.' A closer look at the family might reveal how this can be said.

It has been noted with regard to *The Birthday Party* and *The Caretaker* that Pinter does not begin a play with any exposition or prolonged introduction to the characters and the setting. So when Max begins to insult and threaten either Lenny or Sam our attention is naturally drawn to the immediate relationship being portrayed on stage. However, the background to the family does emerge in great detail as the play proceeds, and a picture of the routine and relationships within the family is well established before the arrival of Teddy and Ruth. In fact the animosity that is displayed throughout the play hides much of what is normal. It is evident that the family live in a well-regulated household which is nothing like a slum. It has always been the family home, once lived in by Max and Sam's parents. Max was a butcher – a trade that insists on cleanliness – and it is likely that the house reflects this. There are clean sheets in the guest room if needed; the dishes are washed. It is not a poor home; Lenny drives an Alfa Romeo, three of the men are employed and Max very probably has money put aside. If he wears old clothes it is for the sake of comfort. The men rise early and work. Max does the cooking. A very distinguishing feature, of course, is the absence of a woman in the house, and the furnishings probably reflect this. Indeed the size of the room has been determined by the death of the mother. As Teddy explains to Ruth:

> TEDDY: What do you think of the room? Big, isn't it? It's a big house. I mean, it's a fine room, don't you think? Actually there was a wall, across there . . . with a door. We knocked it down . . . years ago . . . to make an open living area. The structure wasn't affected, you see. My mother was dead. (p. 23)

This is a significant detail, as all details are significant in a Pinter play. Why was the wall knocked down? With the loss of a family member, why the need for *more* space? This suggests how dominant a presence Jessie was when she was alive. The domestic atmosphere after her death was probably too claustrophobic for the men. The house now is as they like it.

This is a very close family. They interact on a daily basis. The male culture is emphasised by the passing references to sport: to horse racing ('What do you think of Second Wind for the three-thirty?' is a genuine enquiry from Lenny to Max), to football ('I'm going to see a game of football this afternoon. You want to come?' Max asks Joey), and to Joey's boxing. Max goes to the gym with Joey. Also we learn that Lenny has been cruising for women with Joey.

The vital question that really is the key to *The Homecoming* must be, given the grotesque abuse that emanates from Lenny and Max: why do they all stay together? They don't have to. One answer is that they are, essentially, a family and they love each other, they need each other. The same answer, seemingly improbable, might be given to the same question with regard to Eugene O'Neill's *Long Day's Journey Into Night*, in which the parents and two sons spend four long acts in withering denunciation of each other, blaming each other for all the disasters of their lives. They remain together because they are family and they love each other. This basic fact, which is never discussed in *The Homecoming*, is the underlying truth (the subtext, to put it crudely) that explains Max's reaction on first seeing Teddy and Ruth, and Lenny's reaction to them throughout. Teddy is the eldest son of the family and he has betrayed them in the most appalling manner. His disappearance to America and abandonment of the family must, during his six years of absence, have caused the deepest resentment to boil and fester. This alone would make his surprise appearance the cause of passionate and complex emotions. The appearance of Ruth merely compounds his offence. Max doesn't know who she is, and doesn't in the least care. All his fury and frustration is directed at Teddy. If Max recovers enough to 'let bygones be bygones' and cook the family a very good lunch, Lenny is not so forgiving. He is going to make Teddy answer for his betrayal, and Ruth provides the most convenient opportunity.

Ruth and the family

It is generally agreed that although Teddy returns to his family in *The Homecoming* it is Ruth who really comes home. It is also fairly obvious that Ruth is more than a match for all of the men in the play, so we may conclude that she decides to stay in this home of her own free will. As she says when Lenny and Max agree to her demands, 'Yes, it sounds a very attractive idea.' This could be her way of rejecting and putting-down Teddy who has, outrageously, put the proposition to her in the first place. However, all her speeches and actions during Act Two indicate her rejections of her American home and her willingness to engage sexually with Joey and Lenny. There is nothing to stop her returning to America with Teddy, so why does she choose to stay?

Of all the characters in the play Ruth is by far the most enigmatic and she is, of course, the only woman. Her position as the one woman makes her the centre of attention in all her scenes. However, as a dramatic character she takes on an increasingly symbolic status, embodying various male perceptions of 'woman', seen variously as a wife, a mother, a sister, a daughter and a whore. These roles are united in the final stunning image of her, seated and relaxed, in control of the family and the room. So Ruth is both a psychologically realised personality and a symbol of a poetic vision – a representative of 'woman' and a dream-image of male wish-fulfilment.

To begin with, however, it is well to appreciate that it is very difficult for an actor to play a symbol. The character comes first. Ruth is, essentially, the wife brought back to England by her husband to visit his family, and thus may be regarded as the conventional Pinter intruder, whose arrival disturbs the inhabitants of the room and creates the action of the play. She may also be regarded as a *shiksa* – that is a non-Jewish wife who has attracted her husband away from the Jewish family. This family is not definitively Jewish, despite the idiom and rhythm of the language; nevertheless, this marriage has certainly upset the family because they were excluded from it and Teddy has left the family home. So Ruth becomes a means whereby the family can get back at the eldest son for his betrayal. She is central to the 'game' that is intended to belittle Teddy. However, Ruth has her own agenda, which on one level is quite straightforward – she prefers what the family has to offer to what America and Teddy have to offer.

On her arrival in the house with Teddy, after the family have gone to bed, it is evident that the two are estranged. Teddy appears anxious that Ruth be at ease and not nervous, but it is Teddy who is anxious and Ruth who seems perfectly 'at home'. Her question, 'Do you want to stay?' indicates her intuition that this is not a good place for them both to be. Her decision to go for a walk alone (in a London suburb, at night) is very telling. It shows her independence and it also indicates that she knows her way about – later she says, 'I was born quite near here.' It soon emerges that she has absolutely no regard for her life in America. Whenever Teddy tries to impress the family with his success she says nothing. Teddy's account of Ruth's adjustment sounds desperate:

> She's a great help to me over there. She's a wonderful wife and mother. She's a very popular woman. She's got a lot of friends. It's a great life at the University . . . you know . . . it's a very good life. We've got a lovely house . . . we've got all . . . we've got everything we want. It's a very stimulating environment. (p. 67)

But this could be seen as Teddy trying to convince Ruth as much as the family. Her own opinion of America is far from enthusiastic:

It's all rock. And sand. It stretches . . . so far . . .
everywhere you look. And there's lots of insects there.
   Pause.
And there's lot's of insects there. (p. 71)

When Lindsay Duncan played Ruth at the National
Theatre in 1997, she gave this repetition a heart-rending
emphasis. So much for America and – as Lenny scathingly
describes it – 'the old campus'. Later she confides to
Lenny, in what may be assumed as a request to stay:

> RUTH: I'm fond . . .
>   *Pause.*
>   What do you think of my shoes?
> LENNY: They're very nice.
> RUTH: No, I can't get the ones I want over there.
> LENNY: Can't get them over there, eh?
> RUTH: No . . . you don't get them there. (pp. 76–7)

Finally, she rejects Teddy's claim that 'it's cleaner there'
and it is clear that her life in America, and her life with
Teddy, has lost all meaning and appeal.

Her self-confidence and sexual confidence are demon-
strated in her response to Lenny's violent and threatening
speeches in Act One, and in her cool reaction to Max's
filthy assault on her when he first sees her the morning
after her arrival. Her reaction might be contrasted with
that of Cressida when she too is thrown into the lion's
den – the camp of the Greek generals in Shakespeare's
Troilus and Cressida. Cressida very quickly takes up
with Diomedes, whom she twice calls 'guardian'. Ruth
doesn't need a guardian. She is able to look after herself
simply by exercising her sexuality. When she draws
attention to herself and away from Lenny's attempt to

humiliate Teddy over the subject of 'philosophy' she is very explicit:

> Look at me. I . . . move my leg. That's all it is. But I wear . . . underwear . . . which moves with me . . . it . . . captures your attention. (p. 71)

It certainly captures Joey's attention, but it literally scares Max and Lenny out of the room:

> MAX *stands.*
>
> MAX: Well, it's time to go to the gym. Time for your workout, Joey.
>
> LENNY: *(standing)* I'll come with you.
>
> JOEY *sits looking at* RUTH.
>
> MAX: Joe.
>
> JOEY *stands. The three go out.* (p. 72)

Ruth is comfortable in the room and knows that she is wanted and even needed. As soon as she decides to exert her presence she is effortlessly in command:

> RUTH: I'd like something to eat. (*To* LENNY) I'd like a drink. Did you get any drink?
>
> LENNY: We've got drink.
>
> RUTH: I'd like one, please.
>
> LENNY: What drink?
>
> RUTH: Whisky.
>
> LENNY: I've got it.
>
> *Pause.*
>
> RUTH: Well, get it.
>
> LENNY *goes to the sideboard, takes out bottle and glasses.* JOEY *moves towards her.*
>
> Put the record off.
>
> *He looks at her, turns, puts the record off.*
>
> I want something to eat. (pp. 81–2)

In a play that piles shock upon shock one of the most shattering events is the proposition by Lenny that they put Ruth on the game – make a prostitute of her – to save on the expense of keeping her in the house. In the final sequence of the play, Ruth is again the dominant force, driving a hard bargain. The process is ambiguous and remains so to the end. How serious is Lenny's proposal? In the original 1965 Royal Shakespeare Company's production the actors were convinced that Lenny and Max were testing Teddy to the limit – using the absent wife (Ruth is upstairs) to rile him. The suggestion that Ruth should be made a whore was not intended to be carried through. Lenny and Max are trying to outdo each other in shock. If this were to be the case then there is a devastating reversal when Ruth actually agrees by asking, 'How many rooms would this flat have?' At least two responses can be made to this. Firstly, that Ruth has come full circle and is intent on returning to her earlier life as a whore (which we are tempted to believe by her telling Lenny that she used to be 'a photographic model for the body' – meaning, possibly, a prostitute. She also says at one point, 'I was . . . different . . . when I met Teddy . . . first'.) This would be another kind of homecoming – with Ruth replacing Jessie, the former mother/whore of the household.

Alternatively, Ruth could be joining in the 'game' more fiercely. After all, it is Teddy her husband – not Lenny – who says, 'But Ruth, I should tell you . . . that you'll have to pull your weight a little, if you stay. Financially. My father isn't very well off.' So this agreement on her part could be the final pay-off to Teddy – with Ruth giving every appearance of accepting the life of a whore, but with no intention of doing so. It also establishes her total independence from the family. She gets exactly what she wants:

> RUTH: I'd need an awful lot. Otherwise I wouldn't be content.
> LENNY: You'd have everything. (p. 109)

Certain facts are incontrovertible at the end. Teddy leaves, and he leaves Ruth behind. But what Ruth is going to do is not certain:

> MAX: I don't think she's got it clear.
> *Pause.*
> You understand what I mean? Listen, I've got a funny idea she'll do the dirty on us, you want to bet? She'll use us, she'll make use of us, I can tell you! I can smell it! You want to bet?
> *Pause.*
> She won't . . . be adaptable! (pp. 115–16)

The final stage-picture is dense with possible meanings. As such, it is poetic because it reverberates beyond any literal meaning that can be placed on it. A simple view could be that they have all come home to what they want. Joey has a mother, Max has a wife, Lenny has a whore and Ruth has everything. But Ruth remains as enigmatic as the Mona Lisa. We don't know what is going on in her head or what she will do, how she will live. From a symbolic or mythological viewpoint she has been seen as a fertility goddess, bringing new life and redemption to a barren landscape. From a psychoanalytical viewpoint she, as a woman, fulfils the subconscious or dream-wishes of the males of the family. From a sociological viewpoint she is the victor in a struggle for territory: she has taken over the room. Finally, she dominates the stage

with the most powerful and enigmatic of Pinter devices –
silence.

Undoubtedly part of the shock that was generated by
The Homecoming in 1965 is to be found in Ruth's
decision to leave her husband and three children and to
make herself available to other men, even, possibly, to
become a prostitute. This sexual 'liberation' would have
appeared perverse in the extreme to a typical middle-class
audience seeking an uplifting experience from the Royal
Shakespeare Company in 1965. Nora walks out on her
family, and out of the door, at the end of Ibsen's *A Doll's
House*, and, shocking as this was at the end of the nineteenth century, the action is easily understood these days;
it was the sexual dimension of *The Homecoming* that
made the play so disturbing when it was first performed.

Pinter had presented a number of alluring female
characters in earlier plays, where a degree of enigma and
titillation surrounded their sexuality. These included The
Girl in *A Night Out*, Stella in *The Collection* and Sarah in
The Lover (all played by Vivien Merchant). But there was
nothing in these plays to compete with the overt sexual
behaviour and language of *The Homecoming*, nor did
these women command the same power as Ruth, who
must be seen as an exceptional figure for her time. The
whole feminist movement that began to proliferate in the
1970s has changed our perspective on women altogether.
In 1982, Caryl Churchill presented a large number of
contemporary women characters in her play *Top Girls*.
One of them is Louise, aged forty-six, who laments that
she is being overtaken by a younger generation of professional women who are infinitely more liberated than she
could ever be:

I did take on this young woman, her qualifications were excellent, and she did well, she got a department of her own, and left the company for a competitor where she's now on the board and good luck to her. She has a different style, she's a new kind of attractive well-dressed – I don't mean that I don't dress properly. But there is a kind of woman who is thirty now who grew up in a different climate. They are not so careful. They take themselves for granted. I have had to justify my existence every minute . . . (*Top Girls*, II. iii)

Louise would have been a contemporary of Ruth, and quite uncomprehending of her behaviour. In the 1960s, women's roles were still very clearly defined, and the home was sacrosanct. In the 1980s, however, the most popular play in London was Christopher Hampton's adaptation of *Les Liaisons Dangereuses*, at the centre of which is La Marquise de Merteuil. For several years this character dominated the London stage, controlling her social world (in late eighteenth-century France) with a total disregard for morality, especially sexual morality. She does come a cropper in the end, but there was much fascination in her Machiavellian recognition of how people can and do behave, regardless of 'official' morality. Pinter's creation of Ruth in the 1960s was thus far ahead of its time, both in its recognition of a 'free' woman and in its refusal to pander to theatrical 'good taste'.

The human jungle

A famous comment by one of the first people to see *The Homecoming* referred to the characters as behaving just like animals: the implication being that the play was not suitable for civilised human beings. But human beings are animals, albeit cerebral animals and, most distinctively, they are the animals who talk. Dramatic representation of people as animals is generally pejorative and unflattering, implying that animals are, by definition, *sub*-human. Goneril and Regan, the evil daughters in Shakespeare's *King Lear*, are shown to move further and further away from civilised behaviour and are increasingly associated with animal imagery (in contrast to Cordelia, who is angelic). Caliban, in *The Tempest*, is a creature of unrestrained physical appetite and 'this thing of darkness', this 'monster', is regarded as being beyond the benefits of education and nurture. Jonson's characters in *Volpone* are comically associated with animals because of their overriding and aggressive greed, their parasitic qualities. Pinter's *The Homecoming* is unrestrained in its recognition of irrational instinct as being a part of the human condition. People are not entirely subject to the laws of decency, 'civilisation' and good manners, are not always in control of their emotions. The sight is not pretty.

The initial reaction of Peter Hall, the first director of *The Homecoming*, on reading the play was that it 'looks unblinkingly at life in the human jungle' and that 'There's something deeply animalistic about the people's reactions to each other and the way they treat each other' (*Lahr*, p. 9). Hall goes on to say that 'there is a pressure of emotion and an ugliness of motive which I think is a new note in his work'. So Hall is equating 'animalistic' with 'the jungle' and linking the two with an experience which is 'ugly'. A similar judgement was offered by Steven Grant, who claimed that this is 'a play about how families feed off themselves in a cannibalistic ritual' (*Time Out*). In support of these interpretations one could note that fundamental animal instincts are expressed: the instinct for survival, the aspiration to dominate the pack, the fear and resentment of outsiders, the mindless and instinctive drive to kill (as a fox in a henhouse kills everything in sight, not just what it needs for food); the animal instinct for indiscriminate sexual mating is also relevant.

To a certain extent the behaviour of the characters in *The Homecoming*, most notably in their aggression, accords with this kind of animal behaviour. Max was a butcher, and he and MacGregor clearly revelled in being 'two of the worst hated men in the West End', which easily suggests a background of violence. Much of Max's language is violently aggressive. This violence is continued in the family through Joey being a fighter and, more disturbingly, in Lenny's fantasies of violence against women – 'So I just gave her another belt in the nose and a couple of turns of the boot and sort of left it at that' and 'I just gave her a short-arm jab to the belly.' The conflict of generations, Max against his sons, is very primitive. The leader of the family is growing old and is threatened by the younger members of the pack. He is ferocious in defence of his position. Lenny, Teddy and Joey no longer fear him. Ruth and Teddy are 'outsiders' whose threat is greeted by outright attack. Both the male response to Ruth on the sexual front, and her own sexual allurement, consciously and provocatively directed at the men, are basically instinctive.

Max, in particular, fills the play with animal imagery. He claims, early on, to have had 'an instinctive understanding of animals' and 'I always had the smell of a good horse. I could smell him.' His profession involved chopping up animals, carving carcasses: 'I worked as a butcher all my life, using the chopper and the slab, the slab, you know what I mean, the chopper and the slab!' Lenny accuses him of bringing this animal interest into the house: 'You're a dog cook. Honest. You think you're cooking for a lot of dogs.' But Max has already claimed, 'They walk in here every time of the day and night like bloody animals.' Lenny, Teddy, Sam and Jessie are all referred to by Max as 'bitch'; Sam is also an 'old grub' and 'a maggot'. MacGregor is a 'runt'. Finally, Max claims of Ruth that 'She'll make us all animals' – a comment which carries an unconscious irony, given the way they have behaved.

A comedy of bad manners?

The Homecoming is full of charged emotion, aggressive language and tense clashes of personality. The fact that the embattled characters belong to the same family adds a shocking edge to their disputes. Much of the time the audience are not sure what lies behind the animosity. Any past history that might be responsible for the deep well of resentment remains, largely, unknown. This doubt about the past has led some productions of the play to make positive decisions. Characters have been shown to behave as a result of some definite event in the past. The result has been to make the play very dark indeed, and this is probably a mistake. Two examples of interpretations that were possibly misguided relate to the recent and distant past. One assumed that Ruth has been seriously ill, and is suffering a profound mental disorder. This distorted all her scenes because, in fact, she is usually in control. The other production justified the conflict of generations by deciding that the sons had been the victims of child abuse inflicted by the father. This rendered the household very bleak and as hopeless as that of Ibsen's *Ghosts*. A lighter touch is more appropriate, and a clue here is to recognise how funny the play is at times. The characters are not trying to be funny – the wit is entirely Pinter's – but there are some good jokes, very witty speeches and potentially humorous situations. How far these are recognised may depend on one's sense of humour. It has been claimed that there is a hideous side to Pinter's humour in this play and that the comedy is grotesque. It is, however, possible to see *The Homecoming* as a modern comedy of manners. If so, then it is certainly a comedy of bad manners.

There is, for example, a degree of wit in most of the verbal abuse that is exchanged in the play, and humour in our recognition of the exposure of home truths. Obscenity can be the most natural form of expression, even in domestic settings. Invariably it is used for emphasis, and that alone. Max even turns it on himself, without thinking, when Lenny tells him to shut up:

> MAX: Listen! I'll chop your spine off, you talk to me like that! You understand? Talking to your lousy filthy father like that! (p. 3)

Sam lacks the venom of Max, but there is clearly a laugh to be gained from the juxtaposition of statements when he describes MacGregor: 'He was a lousy stinking rotten loudmouth. A bastard uncouth sodding runt. Mind you, he was a good friend of yours.' There is also humour in Max's declaration when Sam comes in and at first ignores him, talking only to Lenny:

> MAX: I'm here, too, you know.
> SAM *looks at him.*
> MAX: I said I'm here, too, I'm sitting here. (p. 8)

Lenny says many things that are set up for a laugh in the theatre, such as his reference to Joey when he is challenging Teddy about his subject:

LENNY: Well, for instance, take a table.
 Philosophically speaking. What is it?
TEDDY: A table.
LENNY: Ah. You mean it's nothing else but a table.
 Well, some people would envy your certainty,
 wouldn't they, Joey? (p. 70)

The likelihood is that Joey would double-take in response to his name, not having a clue what Lenny is talking about. And when Ruth is beginning to confide in Lenny on an intimate level, his answers are wonderfully evasive. When she says that she had been a model before she went away his reply is 'Hats?' and when she is more specific, 'No . . . I was a model for the body. A photographic model for the body', his further reply of 'Indoor work?' is another deliberate evasion that an audience should find amusing.

There is also a comic dimension to much of the game-playing that goes on, i.e. when one member of the family is deliberately trying to belittle another, usually in front of other people. This 'taking the piss' involves asking a straight question with a total lack of sincerity. Lenny is good at it. For example, asking Sam, who has been boasting about how good a chauffeur he is, 'I bet the other drivers tend to get jealous, don't they, Uncle?' is pure mischief. Similarly, testing Teddy in front of the family about his academic subject is totally insincere. He begins, 'Eh, Teddy, you haven't told us much about your Doctorship of Philosophy. What do you teach?' The question might be absolutely genuine, but it isn't. He wants to make Teddy look a fool. This 'attack', couched in apparently sincere language, is developed later, after Teddy has taken Lenny's cheese roll (another blatantly comic device). Lenny delivers a lengthy speech, wholly ironic, using all Teddy's own phrases against him:

> It's funny, because I'd have thought that in the United States of America, I mean with the sun and all that, the open spaces, on the old campus, in your position, lecturing, in the centre of all the intellectual life out there, on the old campus, all the social whirl, all the stimulation of it all, all your kids and all that . . .
> (p. 87)

This insulting of 'guests' by game-playing or use of irony has a comic heritage: it is the basis of Noël Coward's *Hay Fever*, and is central to the witty, and partly comic, *Whose Afraid of Virginia Woolf?* by Edward Albee.

In a brilliant essay, Margaret Croyden (*Lahr*, pp. 45–56) draws comparisons between *The Homecoming* and the comedy of manners of the late seventeenth century, noting the essential and vivid difference – that the social world of *The Homecoming* is lower-middle class and the conscious artifice of speech and behaviour in Congreve or Wycherley is reduced in Pinter's play to almost bestial realism. Remarkably, Croyden draws comparisons between the 'gay couple' of Restoration Comedy and Lenny and Ruth. The gay couple were consciously superior to the other characters and in close collaboration with each other's ideals. So it is possible to compare the marriage 'bargain' and 'contract' negotiated between Mirabell and Millamant (in Congreve's *The Way of the World*) with the contract drawn up by Lenny and Ruth at the end of *The Homecoming*.

Finally, it is possible to argue that the most outrageous moments of *The Homecoming* have a comic dimension because of their sheer absurdity. For example, the family's ignoring the seemingly dead Sam, collapsed on the floor – 'A corpse? A corpse on my floor? Get him out of here!' – is reminiscent of Joe Orton. On the one hand it is quite outrageous; on the other, the best thing to do with someone who has fainted is to leave him alone.

A sick enterprise?

It would be naive to consider the history and the reception of *The Homecoming* without some recognition of the dissenting voices who have argued against it. Most reviewers consider that the unpalatable facts in the play are presented with profound psychological and emotional truth. However, much-respected commentators have objected to the play on the grounds both of dramaturgy (the skill of playmaking) and the limited vision of the playwright. Their arguments can be refuted, but they are worth considering. Firstly Simon Trussler, in a book-length study of Pinter, disapproved of *The Homecoming*. He sees a skilful playwright reduced to the refinement of his own dramatic clichés in a play that is, ultimately, pornographic; and he finds the events of the play improbable. His argument is summed up as follows:

> *The Homecoming* is, in short, a modishly intellectual-ised melodrama, its violence modulated by its vague-ness, its emotional stereotyping disguised by carefully planted oddities of juxtaposition and expression. To suspend disbelief in this play is to call a temporary halt to one's humanity . . . For the characters of *The Homecoming* I, at least, can feel nothing, other than an occasional shock of surprise or disgust: and even these shocks are subject to a law of rapidly diminishing returns. (*Casebook*, p. 185)

The critic Harold Hobson, Pinter's early champion who was the only one to recognise the qualities of *The Birthday Party* in 1958, revelled again in the language and the cleverness of *The Homecoming* but he, also, had reservations about the play:

> I am troubled by the complete absence from the play of any moral comment whatsoever. To make such a comment does not necessitate an author's being conventional or religious; it does necessitate, however, his having made up his mind about life, his having come to some decision . . . we have no idea what Mr Pinter thinks about Ruth or Teddy, or what value their existence has. They have no relation to life outside themselves. They live: their universe lives: but not the universe. If they have a connection with it we are not shown what it is.

'They have no relation to life outside themselves' is a very neat definition of existentialism, and Pinter has been called an existentialist playwright. Perhaps he *is* engaged in an on-going process, as a dramatist, of 'making his mind up' about how his characters live. If the vision is bleak and unedifying it is, none the less, a genuine insight. Pinter has become, over the years, increasingly involved in issues of human rights and political oppression and he has stated his opinion that the world is, in large part, 'a pretty appalling place'. His early plays, including *The Room, The Birthday Party, The Dumb Waiter, The Caretaker* and *The Homecoming*, are centred among mid-twentieth-century urban living, and they present a consistent vision of competitiveness, loneliness and isolation in a threatening world. Because they deal with characters from the working class, or lower-middle class, who make not the slightest claim to heroic or noble status, the complaint is voiced that they have 'grubby souls' and are not worthy of serious consideration. This is to judge the plays by standards that no longer apply. John Lahr's opinion refutes the argument completely: 'The gorgeousness of *The Homecoming* rests with its elusive, hard truth. Pinter is wrestling with his own sense of spiritual dislocation and finding mirrors for ours.' (*Lahr*, p. xviii)

Characters

MAX Max is a commanding presence throughout *The Homecoming*, made so by his ferocious verbal aggression which is directed at everybody in turn. His violent fury derives entirely from the fact of his growing old, and Max is well worthy of a place in the pantheon of dramatic characters who have defined the frustrating experience of ageing. Shakespeare's Prospero (*The Tempest*), Ibsen's Solness (*The Master Builder*), Miller's Willy Loman (*Death of a Salesman*) and Beckett's Ham (*Endgame*) are all studies in old age, and all resent the experience. The greatest example, King Lear, before experiencing the full and awful truth, says ironically, 'I confess that I am old: Age is unnecessary' (II. iv. 152–3). Max is at a stage in life where the past is as much a torment as a comfort because it highlights his present deficiencies. Dylan Thomas famously invoked his dying father, 'Do not go gentle into that good night' because 'Old age should burn and rave at close of day.' This is what Max does throughout the play.

Max hates growing old and the key to his character is resentment. He resents the memory of Jessie because she has died and left him to run the house ('I gave her the best bleeding years of my life, anyway'). He resents Sam because Sam hasn't lived and Max now has to cook for him ('I gave birth to three grown men! All on my own bat. What have you done? *Pause.* What have you done? You tit!'). Most of all he resents his sons, because they are in the process of replacing him, and they are an ever-present reminder of what he has lost. Lenny is smart and independent, Joey is virile and goes training to box, while Max is consigned to the kitchen. His bitterness erupts whenever he is reminded of his own decline, mostly in vicious verbal assaults, but also physically – he punches Joey *'with all his might'* when Joey calls him an old man, exposing his fear of impotence. His furious reaction on seeing Teddy and Ruth for the first time is the result of complex emotions. Teddy is his eldest son who, as such, holds an immeasurable attachment. However Teddy has abandoned his family for six years, so causing an immeasurable disappointment. He has also brought a woman into the house, which nobody has done before. The shock of seeing the two is compounded in Max's mind by the instinct that he has somehow been set up – and that the others know of the arrival, so adding to his humiliation:

> MAX: Did you know he was here?
> *Pause.*
> I asked you if you knew he was here.
> JOEY: No.
> MAX: Then who knew?
> *Pause.*
> Who knew?
> *Pause.*
> I didn't know.

TEDDY: I was going to come down, Dad, I was going
to . . . be here, when you came down.
Pause.
How are you?
Pause.
Uh . . . look, I'd . . . like you to meet . . .
MAX: How long you been in this house?
TEDDY: All night.
MAX: All night? I'm a laughing stock. How did you get
in?
TEDDY: I had my key.
MAX *whistles and laughs.* (pp. 53–4)

Stuck in the house all day, with every day's routine the
same, Max is obsessed with reviving the past when he
believes he was impressive. But the memories are always
double-edged. He boasts about his gift with horses – 'You
only read their names in the papers. But I've stroked their
manes, I've held them, I've calmed them down before a
big race. I was the one they used to call for' – but he was
never actually employed on the racecourse; he was a
fearful figure when seen with MacGregor – 'We were two
of the worst hated men in the West End of London' – but
MacGregor turns out to have had an affair with Jessie,
Max's wife; he entered into negotiations with a top-class
group of butchers with continental connections, but they
turned out to be criminals; he has sentimental memories
of the happy family when the boys were young, but now
the family are a torment to him.

Yet despite these disappointments, and despite the
frustrations of becoming old, Max remains a formidable
figure because of his mental vitality and verbal energy. His
vivid, abusive rhetoric is a rich addition to the play.

LENNY Lenny is the most provocative character in the play, initiating the direction of the dialogue in most of his scenes. However, his motives remain inscrutable: he never explains them, and we can only hypothesise from what he says and does. Even his 'occupation' remains uncertain. There can be no doubt about Max and the butcher's shop or Sam and his cars or Joey in demolition: they talk about their jobs and nobody questions what they say. Lenny admits that he has an occupation, and eventually claims to have 'a number of flats' in the area of Greek Street, by which it is suggested that he is running prostitutes as a pimp. This comes as a surprise to Max, so the matter is at the very least questionable; but we don't in the end need to know – our lack of certainty is part of the intrigue of the play. What holds our interest and what matters is how Lenny behaves on stage. Generally he reacts to rather than creates a situation: he reacts to Max at the beginning of the play, to Sam when he enters, and then to the arrival of Teddy and Ruth. Firstly, he encourages Teddy to go to bed and then awaits the return of Ruth from her walk. Their scene is a remarkable conflict. Lenny's two long monologues fail to impress Ruth in any way. Much speculation has been prompted by Lenny's concern when she calls him 'Leonard':

LENNY: Don't call me that, please.
RUTH: Why not?
LENNY: That's the name my mother gave me. (p. 42)

We can only guess the reason for this response: is Lenny deeply resentful of his mother, and has he developed mysogynistic tendencies as a consequence? His treatment of Ruth is a complex development. At first he tries to dominate her, then he uses her as a means of humiliating

Teddy, then he responds to his recognition that hers is a broken marriage. At the end he hands her over to Joey and the play ends with:

> *She continues to touch* JOEY's *head, lightly.*
> LENNY *stands, watching.*

Lenny has been largely responsible for this conclusion, but it has not been planned or calculated, despite his undoubted cleverness.

Ultimately it is an unrewarding task to try to explain Lenny fully. He shows hostility and is manipulative; he is a bundle of suppressed violence; and he has a degree of independence. He is, like Max, a force in the house, where he survives through his brilliant facility with language, which he uses with great dexterity.

SAM Sam has been regarded as the conscience of the family, the sweet old uncle who does his best to keep the peace and who finally blurts out his guilty secret only to stop what the family are doing to Ruth. But this is surely not the case. He may be the weakest and the most sexless, but he knows how to survive and when he can he is quite prepared to irritate and annoy – Max especially. It is second nature in this family to exploit weaknesses in the others, but in the niggling banter Sam only goes so far. He is shrewd enough to know the limits. If the older generation is under constant threat from the younger, then the two older members – Max and Sam – can also be a constant challenge to each other. Max was tough and has brought up a family, so he can always score against Sam ('What you been doing, banging away at your lady customers, have you?). Sam, however, still has a job and supplies an income, so he can expect Max to cook him a meal – thus emphasising Max's decline in status. His behaviour in the kitchen, noisily washing dishes and clearing up, is certainly a deliberate irritant. The smallest detail can be telling, such as when he first comes in and talks to Lenny. His ignoring Max is a deliberate ploy which hits its mark – Max is forced to proclaim, 'I'm here, too, you know.'

Sam also has the greatest weapon in the armoury of one-upmanship: he knows that Max was cuckolded by MacGregor. Max may well know this, but does he know that Sam knows? Obviously the ground is too dangerous for Sam to dare to exploit openly, but he can regularly bring up the subject of Jessie for his own private mischief. It never fails to rile Max. When he is seen alone with Teddy his motives might be shifty, though he pretends to be a caring confidant. He is prying to see how far he can go with the MacGregor history; he is fishing for a companion in his family line-up, and possibly niggling at Teddy because he stopped writing to him. His shocking outburst about Jessie and MacGregor, which comes out of the blue and knocks him out, is indicative of Sam. He doesn't want the family situation to change as is being proposed – possibly for selfish reasons (he might be replaced by Ruth) – but is too weak to carry through with his challenge. He simply passes out.

TEDDY Commentators on *The Homecoming* are divided about Teddy. Is he the victim or the villain of the play, and does he win or lose? Pinter's objectivity, his intense concern to let his characters speak for themselves, allows us to sit on the fence and say 'both'. On the surface he appears to do badly – he loses his wife to the family, and he suffers a large amount of criticism from Lenny throughout the play. On the other hand it could be argued that Ruth is a wife well worth losing. Of dubious background, mentally unstable and amoral, Ruth might have become an embarrassment to Teddy. Questions are also asked about who the real outsider is in the play, and whose 'homecoming' we see. Again the argument is unclear. On balance, however, if the family has any value at all, then Teddy is the one who opts out. He is the one who proposes to Ruth that she stays and pays her way, while he returns to the arid world of American academe.

Much is made of Teddy's doctorate of philosophy in the play, which is ironic because 'philosophically' is how he reacts to the family – he is determined to remain aloof from the infighting. He is fully aware of how Lenny, and eventually Ruth, are trying to expose his pretentions, but he refuses to be intimidated. When Lenny asks him (in front of all the family) 'Do you detect a certain logical incoherence in the central affirmations of Christian theism?' Teddy knows what Lenny is doing – bluntly, he is taking the piss. Nobody who could frame such a question and put it in this domestic context could be doing anything else. Teddy won't rise to the challenge – 'That question doesn't fall within my province' is his deadpan reply. When Lenny persists, he gets nowhere. Teddy merely states, 'I'm afraid I'm the wrong person to ask' (p. 70). He is equally dismissive when Lenny accuses him, at great length, of letting the side down:

> LENNY: . . . And so when you at length return to us,
> we do expect a bit of grace, a bit of je ne sais quoi,
> a bit of generosity of mind, a bit of liberality of
> spirit, to reassure us. We do expect that. But do we
> get it? Have we got it? Is that what you've given us?

Pause.

TEDDY: Yes. (p. 88)

When Teddy first arrives in the house he is understandably nervous. He projects this anxiety onto Ruth but she is not concerned:

TEDDY: You don't have to go to bed. I'm not saying
   you have to. I mean, you can stay up with me.
   Perhaps I'll make a cup of tea or something. The only
   thing is we don't want to make too much noise,
   we don't want to wake anyone up.
RUTH: I'm not making any noise.
TEDDY: I know you're not. (pp. 25–6)

It isn't stated whether Teddy married Ruth in secret because he was ashamed of her or because he was ashamed of the family. Whichever the case, he knows he is in for a difficult time now that he has brought her home. Seeing her leave the house for a walk, he '*half turns from the window, stands, suddenly chews his knuckles*'. He has real inner concern, but he is not prepared to show it. His first meeting with his brother Lenny establishes the rules immediately. Teddy has been gone for six years, which, as we have noted, must have deeply offended the family, but neither will comment on this obviously shared knowledge. On Lenny's entrance the '*silence*' underlines the fact:

   LENNY *walks into the room from* U.L. *He stands . . .
   He watches* TEDDY. TEDDY *turns and sees him.
   Silence.*
TEDDY: Hullo, Lenny.
LENNY: Hullo, Teddy.
   Pause.

TEDDY: I didn't hear you come down the stairs.
LENNY: I didn't.
  Pause. (p. 28–9)

Teddy epitomises the type of Pinter character whose emotional life is kept hidden. He is no longer able to give expression to it. If we read 'educated' for 'privileged' in this extract from John le Carré, the definition of English dissembling could easily apply to Teddy in the later stages of the play when he refuses to help his wife:

Nobody will charm you so glibly, disguise his feelings from you better, cover his tracks more skilfully or find it harder to confess to you that he's been a damned fool. Nobody acts braver when he's frightened stiff, or happier when he's miserable; nobody can flatter you better when he hates you than your extrovert Englishman . . . of the supposedly privileged classes. He can have a Force Twelve nervous breakdown while he stands next to you in the bus queue, and you may be his best friend, but you'll never be the wiser. (*The Secret Pilgrim*, Hodder and Stoughton, 1991, p. 30)

Teddy will do anything rather than lose face. He tries to articulate his superiority to the rest of the family in his lengthy speech where he argues that he can maintain 'intellectual equilibrium': 'You're just objects. You just . . . move about. I can observe it. I can see what you do. It's the same as I do. But you're lost in it. You won't get me being . . . I won't be lost in it' (p. 84). However, he appears very two-dimensional as a personality in comparison with the other characters in the play. Ruth has clearly recognised this aspect of the campus intellectual who won't live in the real world. In America, Teddy has relegated her to being 'a great help to me over there' – helping with his lectures, looking after the family, being a faculty wife in a surrounding that is, above all else 'clean'. She trips him up on that:

> TEDDY: . . . It's so clean there.
> RUTH: Clean.
> TEDDY: Yes.
> RUTH: Is it dirty here?
> TEDDY: No, of course not. But it's cleaner there. (p. 74)

Teddy wants to keep his hands clean. He won't interfere when his brothers grope his wife because that would show too much concern. He keeps clear of any fight and makes a dignified exit. But it is not impressive. As Peter Hall noted in the performance of Michael Craig, as Teddy, he made the character far from being a martyr or victim: 'He was leaving them with their desserts. He was leaving her with her desserts. And he was the worst of the lot.'

RUTH The fact that Ruth is the one and only woman in *The Homecoming* makes her pivotal, and a touchstone by which we can assess all the men in the play. Furthermore, the archetypal family relationships that are presented allowed her to be seen in symbolic terms as a representative woman: she is regarded by the men in all the variety of roles that a woman can fulfil. However, she is also a character and a personality in her own right, and a complex, enigmatic figure whose motives are uncertain. More than any of the other characters in the play, Ruth commands attention on the stage by the force of her physical presence.

Ruth's magnetic stage presence has generally been

enhanced by the attractiveness, not to say beauty, of the actresses who have played her. She is sexy, and all the men find her physically attractive ('Mind you, she's a lovely girl. A beautiful woman', says Max). Attention is constantly drawn to her by her stage presence and by her movement. This movement is very stylised, to the point where one could imagine the play as a ballet, structured as a series of pas-de-deux. A quality of stillness and self-containment surrounds Ruth, in marked contrast to the passionate emotionalism of the men. The stage directions in the text constantly draw attention to the significance of all her movements. In fact her entire progress can be charted by the choreography of her every move.

She is first seen at night standing with Teddy '*at the threshold of the room*'. The family are asleep.

> RUTH: Can I sit down?
> TEDDY: Of course.
> RUTH: I'm tired.
> *Pause.*
> TEDDY: Then sit down.
> *She does not move.* (p. 21)

In fact she remains standing for some time 'at the threshold', which makes her entry into the room the more expressive. This is the area, the space, the household that is going to change her life and her entry into it is a heightened event. When Teddy finally goes to have a look upstairs, 'RUTH *stands, then slowly walks across the room.*' The instruction '*slowly*' develops the stylised presentation of Ruth – it emphasises the attention that is put on her. Eventually 'RUTH *sits*' and from this static position on stage she is able, physically, to dominate Teddy because the person who is most still on stage generally commands the most attention. She leaves to go for a walk, during which time Lenny prepares to confront her. Then,

> RUTH *comes in the front door.*
> *She stands still.* LENNY *turns his head, smiles. She walks slowly into the room.*

Again the '*slowly*' is stressed. Audience attention is drawn to the slowly moving figure. Again, '*she sits*', and while Lenny delivers his two lengthy and vivid monologues describing his violent confrontations with two women she remains still – and the more still she is the weaker Lenny becomes. And the more forceful is the reaction when she moves:

> *She picks up the glass and lifts it towards him.*
> RUTH: Have a sip. Go on. Have a sip from my glass.
> *He is still.*
> Sit on my lap. Take a long cool sip.
> *She pats her lap. Pause.*
> *She stands, moves to him with the glass.*
> Put your head back and open your mouth (pp. 43–4)

The whole scene is stylised, and Ruth emerges the stronger. Her strength is imposed dramatically by her very controlled and limited movement.

In the morning, when she appears with Teddy and meets the family for the first time, she receives an awful diatribe from Max but maintains her powerful presence by remaining still and not reacting to the violence inflicted on Joey and Sam. When Max talks to her directly she doesn't flinch, but faces him straight on:

> MAX: Miss.
> RUTH *walks towards him.*

RUTH: Yes.

   He looks at her.

MAX: You a mother?

RUTH: Yes.

MAX: How many you got?

RUTH: Three. (p. 56–7)

At the opening of Act Two, after serving coffee, Ruth sits in the midst of the family and from this unmoving position she holds attention whenever she speaks, up to the point when she devastates the male group by drawing attention to her sexuality – 'Look at me. I . . . move my leg. That's all it is. But I wear . . . underwear . . . which moves with me . . .'. Here the very simplest of physical movements can have a tremendous effect in the theatre. The speech focuses all attention on Ruth, but the movement adds significantly to the force of her presence.

When eventually Ruth dances with Lenny, slowly, and kisses him, and when she is then embraced by Joey she says nothing. The effect is very disturbing, mainly because Teddy stands by watching. Ruth's compliance and silence make her next move the more demonstrative. She '*suddenly pushes* JOEY *away*', stands and begins to make demands. She also '*walks around the room*'. This is a stage direction that might easily be slipped over when reading the text, but the walking about the room indicates a degree of taking over – which she is in the process of doing.

Lastly, when she comes downstairs and receives the family's proposition, she is seated throughout until the end, acting as a magnet, until the final tableau shows her in the dominant position, centre stage.

Ruth's movement and her placing on stage help to chart her relationships with the men in the play, but they do not explain her motives. These are never openly disclosed, but they may be inferred from what she says and by how Teddy is presented. Everything points to her choosing to accept the London household for what it is and what it might offer in preference to her past life in America. This argument has been considered above (pp. 143–5), and her use of language will be considered later (p. 182). However, there is a particular feature of her character which has not yet been looked at. Ruth appears somewhat distracted, mentally, as if she were recovering from some crisis. It is typical of Pinter not to make this specific but to offer hints and clues. These come from Teddy, who is concerned for her health: he says, in their first scene, 'You . . . need some rest, you know', and later he is anxious that she should 'rest for a while . . . You can sleep. Rest. Please.' Finally he admits, 'She's not well, and we've got to get home to the children.' She may well have suffered a breakdown brought about by an identity crisis in America where the social demands have made her seriously depressed. After all, as she says. 'I was . . . different . . . when I met Teddy . . . first.' The trip to Italy could then be seen as an attempt at recovery. It didn't work as Teddy might have hoped. As Pinter has said, 'She's in a kind of despair which gives her a kind of freedom. Certain facts, like marriage and family, for this woman have clearly ceased to have meaning.' Her freedom allows her to do exactly as she wants, but we are not told what she is going to do.

JOEY Joey is almost peripheral in the personality conflicts that occur within the family because he has no interest in them and because he is pretty dim-witted. He has none of the brilliance, fluency or cunning that is evident in the others. This leads to a perfectly likely conclusion that he isn't quite part of the same family. His physical strength is evident in his job as a labourer and his ambitions as a boxer (not a very promising prospect), and this presents us with an unsophisticated hefty lump ('that big slag', Max cruelly calls him). He can, therefore, be readily accepted as the son of Jessie. But he is so different from Max, Lenny, Teddy and Sam that circumstantial evidence implies that he could well be the son of MacGregor, the old heavyweight friend of Max who, according to Sam, 'had Jessie in the back of my cab as I drove them along.' It is significant that he is treated almost with affection by the family, probably because he is liked and because he offers no threat to anybody. He is bowled over by Ruth, utterly captivated by her. Clearly he has lived without a mother from an early age and Ruth is something quite different from his usual pick-ups. She opens up a complex and frustrated emotional life which is vividly depicted in the final stage image, reminiscent of the *pietà*, of his lying peacefully in Ruth's lap.

Dramatic Structure

Dramatic structure involves the framework of the play, the ordering of events and the texture of the dramatic material; it involves more than plot or 'forwarding narrative'. In *The Homecoming* there is a central event, which is the return of Teddy with his wife, but the rhythm of the play, which is the vital element in any production, is created by the totality of the structure. Without an understanding of the structure it is unlikely that a production will achieve the right rhythm, and the result would be the equivalent of listening to music played at the wrong speed. In *The Homecoming* structural devices include scenes moving to a climax, and being juxtaposed with scenes of a different tempo; action moving forward according to the psychological development of the characters; and a coherent language, where the repetition of ideas and images keeps the ongoing action tightly related to what has gone before. Most often the rhythm is determined by the way Ruth, in particular, speaks and moves. Here it is necessary to appreciate, as always in reading a good play, that Pinter's writing has a theatrical dimension. It is meant to be spoken and heard in a theatrical space. When this happens, the action takes on a more surreal dimension than might appear on the page.

The play has a linear structure, in that one thing leads to another over a two-day time-span. Characters generally act in accordance with what has just happened to them. A series of dialogues moves towards an emotional climax in a very focused speech followed by a lighting blackout. The scene changes are not of the Shakespearean kind, where all the characters leave the stage for a new group to enter; the progress is more in keeping with musical movements. The first sequence, for example, introduces the family one by one. Lenny is first on stage, quietly checking the runners for the day's horse racing in the paper. He is interrupted by Max, who disturbs him with reminiscences of his success with horses and establishes the niggling banter that is the norm in this household ('did you know that? No, what do you know? Nothing'). Lenny responds to this criticism by damning Max's cooking, and the dialogue very quickly becomes vicious:

LENNY: What did you say?
MAX: I said shove off out of it, that's what I said.

LENNY: You'll go before me, Dad, if you talk to me in
that tone of voice.

MAX: Will I, you bitch?

MAX *grips his stick.* (p. 6)

So Max is fuming when Sam comes in, and having been
threatened by Lenny he turns his anger on the weaker one:

MAX: It's funny you never got married, isn't it? A man
with all your gifts.

Pause.

Isn't it? A man like you?

Then Joey comes in, asking for food. This riles Max even
further, as the cumulative demands on him are allied to
mockery – 'What the boys want, Dad, is your own special
brand of cooking, Dad. That's what the boys look
forward to.' Max's anger and frustration climax in a
speech expressing undisguised hatred for his own father,
followed by a lighting blackout. The scene is dense and
informative. The family are introduced, as are the two
figures Jessie and MacGregor, and the mood of the house
is established. The progress of the scene is structured by
the sequence of entrances in the most natural manner –
both Sam and Joey have returned home from work.

The high emotions of this first sequence are very
suddenly cut dead, and when the lights come up Teddy
and Ruth are standing, silent, at night, looking around the
room. The mood is changed, and with it the rhythm of
the play. The dialogue, filled with pauses, reflects an
emotionally estranged couple and a radical intrusion into
the house. The linear structure continues with Lenny's
reaction to their arrival. He encourages Teddy to go to bed
so that he might confront Ruth. In their blatantly sexual

confrontation Lenny is knocked out of his stride to the extent that he begins shouting, 'What was that meant to be? Some kind of proposal?' The shouting brings Max down and he receives the full force of Lenny's venom. The sequence has again been entirely logical, and again ends with a highly focused, impassioned speech – from Lenny – leading to a lighting blackout. The next movement begins with another change of rhythm: Joey shadow-boxing. Then the progress, as at the beginning, follows a psychologically coherent line involving the increasing anger of Max. Driven out of the kitchen by the noise of Sam washing up, he is then rejected by Joey who won't go with him to a football match. He takes his frustration out on Sam ('What have you done? You tit!') and then explodes on seeing Teddy and Ruth. The act moves to the ambiguous and grotesque face-to-face challenge of Teddy – 'Come on, Dad. I'm ready for the cuddle' and Max's response: 'He still loves his father!'

Throughout the first act the structure has been underpinned by psychological realism. The same could be said of the second act, but it is generally agreed that the play takes on an increasingly surreal dimension as well. A ritualistic texture begins to take over as the balance of power shifts within the family. The movement of the act, which opens with a celebratory family feast (with its own rituals of cigars for the men and coffee all round), shows Ruth becoming absorbed into the family group in a sexual rite. Her 'initiation' is witnessed by Teddy who either withdraws or is excluded from the 'tribe'. On the level of ritual he may be regarded as the scapegoat who has to be sacrificed for the future good of the family/tribe. Ruth becomes both victim and victor. As a woman she takes her place as the necessary symbol of fertility. She also becomes the wish-fulfilment of all the sexual dreams and desires of the men. As many commentators have recognised, the action in Act Two is very ambiguous. It can be taken entirely realistically and naturalistically, i.e. everything happens exactly as we see it. Roger Michell, who directed the play at the Royal National Theatre in 1997, saw it this way, as he describes in an interview:

> I'm approaching this play in a totally naturalistic way. I don't see it as being some kind of essence or abstraction which is being offered up for inspection or examination. I see it as an entirely naturalistic, behavioural account of what happens in a particular house over two days. There's nothing weird about it.

In the theatre, however, the language and movement of Ruth during the second act creates a complexity of responses. They did so in Michell's own production. The structure of the play is determined partly by psychological realism and by elements of ritual, but the play is also held together, poetically, by its verbal echoes. Ideas and phrases reverberate and are repeated tantalisingly throughout. The play begins and ends with Max referring to animals – 'I had an instinctive understanding of animals', and then, about Ruth, 'She'll make us all animals'; also his sense of smell – 'I always had the smell of a good horse. I could smell him. And not only the colts but the fillies.' This is also turned against Ruth at the end – 'She'll use us, she'll make use of us, I can tell you! I can smell it!' Other cross-references include Lenny's mention of 'the Italian campaign' which is used by Ruth against Teddy later on – 'if I'd been a nurse in the Italian campaign'; Teddy's description of his good life in America is thrown back at him, using all his phraseology, by Lenny; Max refers to looking after invalids in the family early and late in the play; Sam as the family 'chauffeur' is a recurrent motif; Jessie and MacGregor, absent characters, are regularly referred to, and the play begins and ends with demands for food and drink. These verbal echoes provide a structural thread, holding the events in a tight, concentrated symmetry.

Language

Language is fundamental to *The Homecoming*. It is the basis of the structure, every scene being determined by how the characters talk and how they use language. The rhythm of the play is controlled by the type of speech patterns employed. Language and speech patterns are also the defining measure of each character. The play uses a stylised naturalistic idiom, a kind of mid-century North London speech, in a variety of forms. This involves abusive, obscene language; monologues that have different impacts and purposes; language games where personal attacks are couched in the strategic use of spurious enquiries – seemingly polite and genuine but really destructive and malicious; cryptic exchanges, where a subtext is at work and a mystery colours what is happening on stage; repetitive imagery which adds a poetic dimension to the play; and juxtaposition of speech patterns (that is, rapid shifts from one form of speech to another).

This variety of linguistic structures is underpinned by two basic criteria: the social background of the characters, which determines the kind of English they speak; and the theatrical dimension, whereby everything that is said happens in a public arena. It is overheard by an audience who are held captive in a space, and who are focused (silently and voyeuristically) on the action on stage and the performance of the actors. All the language is constructed in the light of this primary aesthetic fact: the characters speak on stage.

London speech

Because the play is set in working-class London many commentators loosely describe the language, the natural speech patterns, as 'cockney'. But the written style of the play is in no way a parody or pastiche of cockney accent and idiom, and the extent to which cockney should be emphasised is open to question. A cockney is a native Londoner, traditionally born within the sound of the bells of St Mary-le-Bow in Eastcheap, who speaks with a very distinctive accent which has reached a wide audience through literature and drama. In film, television and theatre, characters have made this regional accent highly distinctive and recognisable. It is the language of *Oliver!*, *Steptoe and Son*, *'Til Death Do Us Part* and *EastEnders*. The characters in *The Homecoming* might well speak with a cockney accent, but the writing makes no insistence on the emphasis. It is more subtle and stylised. For example, early in the play Max says, 'I used to knock about with a man called MacGregor', and then to Lenny, 'shove off out of it'. The expressions 'knock about with' and 'shove off' are idiomatic, colloquial and unsophisticated – associated more with working-class speech. However, the accent employed to pronounce the words 'about' and 'out' can determine the degree of realism/naturalism that is going to be used in the production of the play. A cockney would pronounce these words 'abaht' and 'aht', with a lengthened 'a' and without sounding the 't', but it is possible that to exaggerate the cockney in performance would be to detract from the poetic realism that the play achieves in Act Two. Nigel Williams' play *Class Enemy* is written throughout in colloquial London working-class speech and the difference between his language and that of Pinter is readily apparent:

> IRON: No one done me no favours Nipper an' donch yoo ferget it. No one in this wide world done me no favours right? Right. Now piss off up there an' give us some knowledge. (*Class Enemy*, Faber and Faber, p. 38)

Contrast with this the speech pattern of Max in *The Homecoming*, who speaks with a relish for language and a natural colloquial rhythm, but who is also very precise:

> MAX: He talks to me about horses.
> *Pause.*
> I used to live on the course. One of the loves of my life. Epsom? I knew it like the back of my hand. I was one of the best-known faces down at the paddock. What a marvellous open-air life. (p. 4)

London audiences were much more appreciative of *The Homecoming* than the regional ones who saw the play in preview in 1965, and the strong possibility is that the London audience recognised to a much greater extent the nature of the language and especially how it is used in the play, because it comes from close to home. It is the richness of the language and the personalised aggression that matters, more than an accurate reproduction of exaggerated cockney.

The language of aggression

Sometimes the characters speak to each other in an uncomplicated, straightforward manner, as when Lenny asks Max for a racing tip or when Max tells Joey that he prefers the kitchen to the living room – but these occasions are rare indeed. More often language is used very deliberately as a weapon in order to dominate or humiliate. Characters know what they are trying to achieve, and are equally sensitive to the way language is directed at them. This point is stressed in the opening exchange of the play:

> MAX: Do you hear what I'm saying? I'm talking to you! Where's the scissors?
> LENNY: (*looking up, quietly*) Why don't you shut up, you daft prat?
> MAX *lifts his stick and points it at him.*
> MAX: Don't you talk to me like that. I'm warning you. (p. 2)

Max leads the family in giving vent to his anger and aggression in language of the utmost grossness. The habit is so familiar that it ceases to have any effect. However, shocking it may sound on stage, it simply washes over Lenny:

> MAX: . . . Mind you, she wasn't such a bad woman. Even though it made me sick just to look at her rotten stinking face, she wasn't such a bad bitch. I gave her the best bleeding years of my life, anyway.
> LENNY: Plug it, will you, you stupid sod, I'm trying to read the paper.
> MAX: Listen! I'll chop your spine off, you talk to me like that! You understand? Talking to your lousy filthy father like that!
> LENNY: You know what, you're getting demented.
> *Pause.*

What do you think of Second Wind for the three-thirty? (pp. 3–4)

Everybody is on the receiving end of Max's abuse: Sam ('This man doesn't know his gearbox from his arse'), the family ('One cast-iron bunch of crap after another'), even Ruth ('a stinking pox-ridden slut'). Lenny's aggression is also powerful, but it is much more controlled – as when he turns on Max and asks for details of his own conception (p. 46). The language is calm and rational, but none the less destructive ('I'm only asking this in a spirit of enquiry, you understand that, don't you'). Lenny's reluctance to develop a conversation when he first sees Teddy is a form of controlled aggression. On the one hand he wants Teddy out of the way so that he can meet Ruth, but on the other his lack of interest in his long-lost brother is defiant:

TEDDY: I've . . . just come back for a few days.
LENNY: Oh yes? Have you?
  Pause.
TEDDY: How's the old man?
LENNY: He's in the pink.
  Pause.
TEDDY: I've been keeping well.
LENNY: Oh, have you?
  Pause.
  Staying the night then, are you? (pp. 30–31)

Lenny and Max are both adept at using personal names ironically to insult other members of the family. Whenever Max calls Sam directly by his name it is usually in connection with some accompanying attack; and Lenny's repetition of 'Dad' can easily niggle Max ('What the boys

want, Dad, is your own special brand of cooking, Dad').
Towards the end of the play, when Max and Lenny are
deliberating the future of Ruth, it is really Teddy whom
they are both trying to target and this fact is underlined by
their repeated references to him personally ('What do you
think, Teddy?' . . . 'Eh? Teddy, you're the best judge' . . .
'Listen, Teddy, you could help us' . . . 'No, what I mean,
Teddy . . .'). Similarly, there is an awful irony,
intentionally aimed at Teddy, in Max's mock-concern
regarding Ruth – 'Lenny, do you mind if I make a little
comment? It's not meant to be critical. But I think you're
concentrating too much on the economic considerations.
There are other considerations. There are the human
considerations' (p. 98).

The rhythm of Ruth

The stale pattern of life that has been established by the
male-oriented family after the death of Jessie is completely disrupted when Ruth enters the house. Not only
does she disturb because she is a woman, but she tends to
disrupt all the normal speech patterns of the men every
time she opens her mouth. She creates a very different
rhythm, and this bothers everybody. She certainly adds to
the disturbance of Teddy when they first arrive. Teddy is
nervous anyway, but Ruth continually undermines him
with her deadpan replies:

> TEDDY: . . . Are you cold?
> RUTH: No.
> TEDDY: I'll make something to drink, if you like.
> Something hot.
> RUTH: No, I don't want anything. (pp. 22–3)

and shortly after,

TEDDY: . . . Are you tired?
RUTH: No.
TEDDY: Go to bed. I'll show you the room.
RUTH: No, I don't want to. (pp. 24–5)

She completely devastates Teddy when she decides to go for a stroll, for a breath of air, because this indicates the extent of her independence:

TEDDY: But what am I going to do?
Pause.
The last thing I want is a breath of air. Why do you want a breath of air?
RUTH: I just do. (p. 27)

These brief, undeveloped answers make Ruth the more enigmatic and the more powerful of the two on stage. She employs a similar tactic when she returns from her walk and is confronted by the waiting Lenny. In their remarkable scene (pp. 33–44) Ruth reverses the balance of power by destroying Lenny's verbal rhythm. She wrong-foots him immediately with her first words:

LENNY: Good evening.
RUTH: Morning, I think.
LENNY: You're right there.

Lenny is full of confidence to begin with, ignoring Ruth's claims to being Teddy's wife, and bombarding her with his verbal dexterity and invention. But her one-line responses leave him floundering – 'How did you know she was diseased?' and 'It's not in my way' render his set-piece monologues quite ineffectual. Whenever the men try to overwhelm Ruth with speech, she undercuts them with her own more telling and disturbing responses. Max is utterly deflated following his elaborate and sentimental reminiscence of Jessie and the boys (p. 61) by her one line, 'What happened to the group of butchers?' And when Teddy makes a last desperate plea for her to come home (p. 72) she responds to his lengthy argument with a single line which puts an end to the discussion – 'But if I'd been a nurse in the Italian campaign I would have been there before.'

When Ruth speaks in front of the family she draws attention to her presence by using a different style of delivery, often breaking up her speech with pauses:

RUTH: I was . . .
MAX: What?
    Pause.
    What she say?
    They all look at her.
RUTH: I was . . . different . . . when I met Teddy . . .
    first. (p. 66)

These pauses are also present in her speech which draws attention away from the 'philosophy' debate (p. 71) and when she describes the country house where she used to do her modelling (pp. 77–8). The effect of this stylisation in the theatre is to take the play onto a different level of realism – a more poetic realism.

A mark of Ruth's progress and absorption into the family is the shift in her language at the end when she dominates in the negotiation of a contract, using legal terminology with assured confidence:

RUTH: All aspects of the agreement and conditions
    of employment would have to be clarified to our
    mutual satisfaction before we finalised the contract.
LENNY: Of course. (p. 109)

The physical appearance on stage of an attractive woman, surrounded by a group of men, is bound to create interest. In *The Homecoming*, however, Ruth is able to keep control not only by her sexuality, her physical presence, but also by her use of language.

The Homecoming: In Conclusion

The Homecoming has retained its power to shock by its apparent assault on respectable family values. The aggression and violence shown between the generations, the hatred of women displayed by the disaffected male family, and the ruthless assault on the returning son and his wife are all provocative, disturbing and unpleasant. However, the play also has a powerful theatrical impact, and despite the most obvious complaints that may be levelled at the characters for their language and behaviour, it is possible to find a more positive and hopeful scenario being explored. The play is also much more funny than it might at first appear.

The action revolves around the male family and Ruth. They are all frustrated and in need. The behaviour between them might just as reasonably be related to a concept of love as hate. The family – except for Teddy – have stayed together and acknowledge that they are a unit. The absent mother, Jessie, for all her reputed faults, has left a vacuum. In America, Ruth has been driven to despair by the life that has been imposed on her. The family needs a woman, and the woman wants to be needed. The play moves to a logical conclusion.

Because of the apparent immorality that is displayed during the play and the revelation of what might be called 'basic instincts', the play is bound to disturb and upset.

However the main focus is on basic human needs: the need to be recognised, appreciated, wanted. All the characters, apart from Teddy, reveal their insecurity and expose their emotional weakness. Teddy, who claims to be in control of his life and emotions, is rejected.

Above all, the play is written and shaped for live performance. In the theatre the character of Ruth is elevated by her physical presence and her stylised movement, and becomes increasingly symbolic of what the male psyche seeks in the female. The play begins with a gathering together of a male family, well used to daily in-fighting and superficial abuse. With the introduction of Ruth there begins a ritual of sexual competitiveness which becomes increasingly surreal but concludes in a silent stage-picture which is potently suggestive of what each character most needs.

Textual Notes

Act One

2 daft prat – Lenny begins a sequence of abusive
  terms with which the family address each other.
– These are largely meaningless – the small-change of
  colloquial banter – or gestures of more or less
  aggression. Max in particular uses language very
  aggressively.
– Navy surplus – clothing of the armed forces is sold
  off cheaply when no longer required.
– tearaway – here means someone who could survive
  in the violent suburban world of East London.
3 MacGregor – a Scotsman with whom Max had an
  association in the past. He casts a dark shadow over

the play – as a strong man against whom Sam can
be adversely compared, and as a possible lover of
Jessie, the wife and mother.
- knock about with – associate with.
- still got the scars – from fighting; Max introduces
the theme of violence in the play.
- Plug it – shut up.
- I'll chop your spine off – a violent expletive. The
well-established English vocabulary of four-letter
swear words was forbidden on stage in the 1950s.
Pinter employs a range of vicious and obscenely
abusive phrases which convey aggression and which
brilliantly evaded official censorship because they
were original.
4 Second Wind for the three-thirty – the name of a
racehorse and the time of a race.
5 a few bob – a few shillings: Max says he was a
moderately successful gambler.
6 shove off out of it – move out of the house.
8 Yankee – a dated term for an American.
- Savoy, Caprice – hotel and restaurant in London
frequented by the wealthy.
- Eaton Square – an exclusive area of central
London.
11 Humber Super Snipe – a top-of-the-range luxury car
of the day.
- pass the time of day – make appropriate
conversation.
- Flying Fortress – a large (four-engined) Second
World War American bomber.
12 banging away – engaging sexually.
- crafty reefs – sexual relations.
13 a good bang – sexual intercourse.

- Other people – Sam is evasive, but he is almost certainly referring to Jessie and MacGregor.

14 Dorchester – an expensive London hotel.

16 you bitch – for comment on the animal imagery in the play, see this book, pp. 149–52.

- He used to like tucking up his sons – Lenny's comment is certainly aggressive, but inconclusive; he could be emphasising how old Max has become, or showing deep resentment about how he had been treated.

17 the bag – the punch-bag, used for training in the gymnasium.

18 a bastard uncouth sodding runt – the actor John Normington, who has played Sam twice, argues that Sam is not so adept as Max or Lenny when it comes to verbal assaults.

19 give you the boot – throw you out of the house.

20 cast iron bunch of crap . . . stinking puss – further vivid examples of Pinter's creative obscenity.

- TEDDY and RUTH stand at the threshold of the room – the delay in their actually entering the room is significant; the room is going to become a domestic battlefield and so the intrusion is given heightened emphasis.

28 chews his knuckles – Teddy rarely gives expression to his innermost feelings. This gesture signifies a serious personal crisis.

31 in the pink – in good health.

32 LENNY yawns – here, as always, the stage direction is an important part of the text. By yawning Lenny indicates that he wants to go to bed. In fact he wants Teddy to go to bed, so that he can meet Ruth. This is what happens.

36 chuffed to his bollocks – a common and vivid
colloquial expression which was, nevertheless,
banned in 1965: 'chuffed to his eyeballs' was
substituted.

37 the old man – colloquial for father.

38 the pox – venereal disease.

– clumped her one – hit her.

39 all quiet on the Western Front – the English title of
a novel by the German writer Erich Maria
Remarque, here incorporated naturally into Lenny's
rhetoric.

42 Leonard – the use of personal names, the first mark
of identity, is given heightened significance
throughout the play. Either by repetition or
emphasis, names are frequently used to gain
domination. Ruth, at this point, has found a
weakness.

45 pop off, eh? – this understatement is more forceful
than other more violent terms.

54 Tarts . . . smelly scrubber . . . stinking pox-ridden
slut – Max's obscene abuse is not a direct personal
attack on Ruth so much as a passionate response to
seeing Teddy by surprise after six years, and in the
company of a woman.

55 shacks up – moves into.

Act Two

61 a few bob – a few shillings (spending money).

– pouffe – a large cushion used as a seat or a foot rest.

63 You'd bend over for half a dollar / For two bob
and a toffee apple – Max is implying that Sam
would accept payment for homosexual liaisons –
more as a form of abuse than in actual belief: 'half

a dollar' was colloquial for two shillings and sixpence in old money; 'two bob' was two shillings.

69 Do you detect a certain logical incoherence . . . – Lenny's question is insincere. He knows such a question can make Teddy look foolish if he tries to answer it simplistically (and perhaps more so if he engages philosophically in this household). Teddy doesn't rise to the bait.

– my province – my specialist area of knowledge.

70 the Ritz Bar – part of one of London's most exclusive hotels.

75 But if I'd been a nurse – Ruth rejects the invitation to return home with a line reminiscent of Lenny's speech on p. 37.

77 cloche – the swathe of veiling around a small close-fitting hat.

79 she's wide open – sexually available.

80 rubdown – a massage given to a sportsman after training.

84 intellectual equilibrium – Teddy claims to have the mental capacity to remain above the infighting and personal rancour of the family. Some commentators see the debate between brain and emotion as central to the play.

87 cards on the table stunt – a definitive personal statement.

88 gander – look.

89 je ne sais quoi – I know not what.

– all the way – to sexual consummation.

90 a tease – a woman who provokes sexual interest but doesn't satisfy the desire.

– go the whole hog – reach sexual consummation.

91 dolly – women.

- the Scrubs – Wormwood Scrubs, a prison in West
  London.
94 the gravy – the satisfaction.
96 She's not well – for comment see this book, p. 171.
97–8 a few bob, a few quid – a few shillings (old
  money), a few pounds.
100 on the game – set her up as a prostitute.
- Greek Street – an area of London, in Soho,
  notorious then for lowlife.
102 shoving your oar in – interfering.
103 the Savoy – an expensive London hotel.
- nice quiet poke – discreet sexual liaison.
104 Pan-American – an international airline.
110 *He croaks and collapses* – when asked if Sam is
  dead Pinter replied, 'No, [Sam is] not living any
  more.' He may have had a stroke, or simply fainted.
  His intervention has been too much of a strain and
  he wouldn't have had the strength to follow it up.
112 the six-mile limit – the limit outside central London
  beyond which taxi cabs were permitted to charge
  double fare.
116 *She continues to touch* JOEY's *head, lightly* – for
  comment on the final tableau see this book,
  pp. 147–8.

Chronology of Plays

1957 *The Room* (first performance 1957, University of
Bristol Drama Department, directed by Henry
Woolf; 1960, Hampstead Theatre Club, directed by
Harold Pinter)

      The Dumb Waiter (1960, Hampstead Theatre Club,
directed by James Roose-Evans)

1958 *The Birthday Party* (1958, Arts Theatre, Cambridge,
and Lyric Theatre, Hammersmith, directed by
Peter Wood)

      A Slight Ache (1959, BBC Third Programme,
directed by Donald McWhinnie)

      The Hothouse (1980, Hampstead Theatre, directed
by Harold Pinter)

1959 *The Caretaker* (1960, Arts Theatre, directed by
Donald McWhinnie)

      A Night Out (1960, BBC Third Programme,
produced by Donald McWhinnie)

1960 *Night School* (1960, Associated-Rediffusion
Television, directed by Joan Kemp-Welch)

      The Dwarfs (1960, BBC Third Programme,
produced by Barbara Bray)

1961 *The Collection* (1961, Associated-Rediffusion
Television, directed by Joan Kemp-Welch)

1962 *The Lover* (1963, Associated-Rediffusion
Television, directed by Joan Kemp-Welch)

1964 *Tea Party* (1965, BBC Television, directed by
Charles Jarrott)

The Homecoming (1965, Royal Shakespeare
Company, Aldwych Theatre, directed by Peter
Hall)

1966 *The Basement* (1967, BBC Television, directed by
Charles Jarrott)

1967 *Landscape* (1968, BBC Radio, directed by Guy
Vaesen; 1969, Royal Shakespeare Company,
Aldwych Theatre, directed by Peter Hall)

1968 *Silence* (1969, Royal Shakespeare Company,
Aldwych Theatre, directed by Peter Hall)

1970 *Old Times* (1971, Royal Shakespeare Company,
Aldwych Theatre, directed by Peter Hall)

1972 *Monologue* (1973, BBC Television, directed by
Christopher Morahan)

1974 *No Man's Land* (1975, National Theatre, Old Vic
Theatre, directed by Peter Hall)

1978 *Betrayal* (1978, National Theatre, directed by Peter
Hall)

1980 *Family Voices* (1981, BBC Radio 3, directed by Peter
Hall)

1982 *Victoria Station* (1982, National Theatre, directed by Peter Hall)

A Kind of Alaska (1982, National Theatre, directed by Peter Hall)

1983 *Precisely* (1983, Apollo Theatre, directed by Harold Pinter)

1984 *One for the Road* (1984, Lyric Theatre Studio, Hammersmith, directed by Harold Pinter)

1988 *Mountain Language* (1988, National Theatre, directed by Harold Pinter)

1991 *The New World Order* (1991, Royal Court Theatre Upstairs, directed by Harold Pinter)

Party Time (1991, Almeida Theatre, directed by Harold Pinter)

1993 *Moonlight* (1993, Almeida Theatre, directed by David Leveaux)

1996 *Ashes to Ashes* (1996, Royal Court Theatre at the Ambassadors Theatre, directed by Harold Pinter)

2000 *Celebration* (2000, Almeida Theatre, presented in a double-bill with *The Room*, directed by Harold Pinter)

Select Bibliography

Primary Sources

Pinter's plays are collected in four volumes, published by Faber and Faber. Some of the plays are also available in single editions.

Secondary Sources

There has been an incredible amount written about Pinter, to the extent that twenty years ago a bibliography made a book in itself (Steven H. Gale, *Harold Pinter: An Annotated Bibliography*, Boston: G. K. Hall, 1978); the outpouring of books and articles has not declined since then. The selection given below indicates what is most helpful with regard to the plays dealt with in this volume, and some of the varied approaches to the playwright's work.

Billington, Michael, *The Life and Work of Harold Pinter*, London: Faber and Faber, 1996. The most up-to-date, detailed and authoritative study of Pinter's life and work. It is both very readable and convincing. Billington's original approach is to place the work in the developing context of Pinter's life, so that the plays are shown frequently to connect to the writer's recollections of his own experience. In pursuit of this enquiry Billington was helped invaluably by having

direct contact with Pinter, his wife Lady Antonia
Fraser, colleagues and friends.

Burkman, Katherine H., *The Dramatic World of Harold
Pinter: Its Basis in Ritual*, Columbus: Ohio State
University, 1971. This ingenious reading of the plays
suggests that they are structured according to ritualistic
rhythms. The kings of Frazer's *The Golden Bough* offer
a metaphorical clue to the ritual sacrifices at the centre
of the plays. The scapegoat of ancient ritual and
tragedy may be reproduced as the victim at the centre
of the action of most of Pinter's plays. His destruction
serves to re-establish certain basic relationships in the
family or community. Similarly, Pinter's women can be
seen to relate to fertility goddesses.

Esslin, Martin, *Pinter the Playwright*, London: Methuen,
1973, revised 1992. A standard introduction to Pinter
which has been regularly expanded and revised. It is
authoritative regarding the facts of Pinter's career, and
offers valuable insights into the approach to character
and language. In particular, Esslin regards the plays as
'lyrical images of an unverified, unverifiable and
therefore dreamlike world between fantasy and
nightmare'. Esslin also emphasises the importance of
the subtext.

Gabbard, Lucina P., *The Dream Structure of Pinter's
Plays: A Psychoanalytic Approach*, Cranbury, NJ:
Associated University Press, 1976. The book illuminates
the ambiguity and obscurity of Pinter's plays via a
Freudian concept drawn from *The Interpretation of
Dreams*. The plays become 'dream-texts' where
characters are not unmotivated but unconsciously
motivated. They are grouped around Oedipal wishes,
involving punishment dreams and anxiety dreams. 'The

room' is the key dream, establishing Pinter's convention of the subtext beneath the manifest context of the plots. This daunting subject should not be ignored, as Pinter is highly regarded as an observer of psychoanalytic processes in his plays.

Gale, Steven H., *Butter's Going Up: A Critical Analysis of Harold Pinter's Work*, Durham, NC: Duke University Press, 1977. A standard reference work on Pinter. The book considers the treatment of key themes – love, loneliness, menace, communication and the problem of verification – drawing on a wide array of critical opinion. It is not so good on the plays as works for the threatre but it does contain a comprehensive list of factual detail concerning Pinter's writings, first performances, awards and an extensive bibliography.

Gussow, M., *Conversations with Pinter*, London: Nick Hern Books, 1994. Pinter in five conversations with the drama critic of the *New York Times* held between 1971 and 1993. The rarity of Pinter's public pronouncements makes this a valuable collection. He talks of his priorities in dramatic writing – language, character, rhythm, structure and the nature of time – and distinguishes between his roles as writer and a public/private citizen.

Knowles, Ronald, *Text and Performance, 'The Birthday Party' and 'The Caretaker'*, London: Macmillan, 1988. A sound critical commmentary which examines the language, imagery and action of Pinter's early plays. The theatrical interpretation of the main characters is contrasted in relation to a number of productions.

Lahr, John, ed., *A Casebook on 'The Homecoming'*, New York: Grove Press, 1971. A collection of ten essays on the play and four invaluable interviews with practitioners involved in the original 1965 production of *The Homecoming* by the Royal Shakespeare Company. These are Peter Hall (director), John Bury (designer), John Normington (Sam) and Paul Rogers (Max). Their insights are relevant to Pinter in general, especially from the practical viewpoint.

Page, Malcolm, *File on Pinter*, London: Methuen, 1993. A compilation which includes a detailed performance history of the plays, plot summaries, excerpted reviews and a selection of Pinter's own comments on his work.

Pinter, Harold, *Various Voices: Prose, Poetry, Politics, 1948–1998*, London: Faber and Faber, 1998. Pinter's own selection of his non-dramatic writing covering his whole career.

Scott, Michael, ed., *Harold Pinter: 'The Birthday Party', 'The Caretaker' and 'The Homecoming': A Casebook*, London: Macmillan, 1986. A valuable collection of essays prefaced by a concise summary of critical approaches to Pinter's work. There is a good balance of academic and practical considerations from the best known of Pinter commentators.

Thompson, David T., *Harold Pinter: The Player's Playwright*, London: Macmillan, 1985. Drawing both on Pinter's experience as an actor and the theatre and media of the time, the book argues that his diverse experience contributed directly to the unique quality of his drama. This is useful for suggesting possible sources and influences behind the early plays.